We The Angels

The Star-Born Story of Humanity's Celestial Origins

Howard Reed

DEVORSS *Publications*

© 1998 Howard Reed

ISBN: 0-87516-711-X

Library of Congress Card Catalogue Number: 97-77526

Cover Art:
"The Starseed Mandala"
© 1997 Gage Taylor & Uriel Dana

DEVORSS & COMPANY, *Publisher*
BOX 550
MARINA DEL REY, CA 90294-0550

Printed in the United States of America

To All My Teachers

Thank you for your patience. Thank you for giving me the visions, the ideas and the inspiration that started a flow of verse while listening to Lyssa Royal's *Earth Inception* tapes in May of 1990 and continued until today when it said, "We are done."

Without Orpheus Phylos and Archangel Michael, who introduced me to Raphael, Gabriel and Uriel, I would not have understood the Law of Cessation, and there would be no understanding of Framework Two, Seth, Paula Woolsey and Arbuckle Standish Mc Gee (The Brigadoon). Without Jade Wah'oo, Grandfather Fire, and Grandfather Tobacco, there would be no understanding of our separation from Creator so many aeons ago. It was Robert Shapiro and Zoosh who took my questions about Sirius and Helios and Vesta, and showed me the beginnings of Mother Earth. *"God,"* I thought; *"what a grand plan We live within!"*

It was Rick Royal who, in his incredible way, led me to Lyssa Royal and Keith Priest and the *Earth Inception* tapes, and to the book *The Prism of Lyra.* Here I found the meaning of our Creator's Law of One and the reasons for polarity through Germane, Sasha and Akbar. Lyssa and Keith showed me why! And I am honored to have their permission to take their entire story and add to it my own knowing. I owe *We The Angels* entirely to all of my teachers, my mother, and my wife and companion, Margot, who tirelessly proofed and reproofed each chapter.

****

But before I could meet Margot, Orpheus, Robert, Paula, and Lyssa, I had to meet Kathie and George Butts . It was Kathie who introduced me to Jane Ann Dow and Lucretia. And then there was the Harmonic Convergence, which finally led me to Psynetics in Anaheim, where I thought I was attending a class taught by Margo (without a T) Cheney, the author of the Nicola Tesla biography. SURPRISE, SURPRISE!

Six months later, Margot (with a T) and I stood in front of the blacked-out store in Cottonwood, Arizona, and I decided to open a book and gift shop. The following year we were married. From that time 'til now we have been together, sharing ecstasy, disappointment and sadness as we pushed at the bubble of our confinement, expanding our "We-ness." Together we have met great friends like Dolly, Sherrill, Cile, Jeff, Bob, Betsy, Jim and Jonne, Carol the Angel, Eric the Generous, Shell the Blithe, Mark the Herbalist, Abraham the Kahuna, Ann the Funny, Norman the Healer, and Susan the Gifted.

And finally, I want to thank my mother, who maintained her sharp wit and humor as well as her zest for her personal liberty and freedom throughout all of her life. She taught me more about creating my own realty than all the books and philosophers ever could. Never once did her support waver. Never once did she say it couldn't be done. Without her, *We The Angels* could never have been written or published.

We The Angels is dedicated to the memory of Angel
First Class Phyllis Reed, my mother and the best teacher
anyone could have had.

Flagstaff
May 26, 1996

Contents

Prelude

In that Time before there *was* Time, there was Grandfather Fire. And with him was the Circle of Animal Brothers. It was a good time. A time when the brotherhood of all things was taken for granted. A time when all things were united by their thoughts and their deeds. We wanted for nothing because there was nothing to want. And so it was with our brothers.

Our existence was spent sitting around our Grandfather telling our stories, and beyond us was the Darkness. Each in his turn would tell his Tellings in that sacred language of Spirit, and in so doing give rise to all forms of Creation.

First to speak was brother Eagle,
　　then Raven,
　　　　then Owl,
　　　　　　and then Gander.
Then there was brother Bear,
　　then Panther,
　　　　then Deer,
　　　　　　and then Horse.
Then there was brother Turtle,
　　then Fire Lizard,
　　　　then Snake,
　　　　　　and then Spider.
We, the *Two-Leggeds*, spoke last.

One day, when it was time for us to speak again, our brothers noticed that We were missing. We, the Two-Leggeds, had left the Circle. There was nowhere for us to have gone but into the Darkness. Our brothers could not understand why We had left. Our stories were good. Everyone had liked our Tellings. We were missed. A part of everyone was missing. Each in his own way felt an emptiness.

And so our brothers began to speak about this, and their Tellings, in that sacred language of Spirit, changed. Giving rise to a *new* form of Creation. Our Animal Brothers began to wonder, speaking questions, needing answers.

"Well," asked Turtle Brother, "where are those Two-Leggeds?"

Spider answered, "They were sitting next to me, I saw them get up and walk out there in that Darkness."

"What are they doing out there?" asked Snake.

"I don't know," answered Spider.

"Well, what is this thing, this Darkness that's out there, anyway?" asked Brother Bear. "What is it that calls the Two-Leggeds to leave our Circle and go out there into the Darkness, leaving our Circle open?"

****

The questions continued. Each in his turn, each in his own way, expressing his concern.

Grandfather Fire, hearing their wonderment and the questions that crept into their Tellings, felt the change that the expression of Creation was making. He spoke: *"Here now, Brother Owl. You are my best hunter and seeker of the night. I desire that you go out in the Darkness and look for those Two-Leggeds."*

The Animal Brothers agreed this was a good idea because Owl could see in the Dark. And so Owl stood up and flexed his wings and then quickly flew into the Darkness. He was gone for a long time. Flying this way and that way. Looking and flying, and looking some more. He could see everything there was within his short range. But Owl could not find the Two-Leggeds anywhere. Finally he returned to the Circle of Animal Brothers and said, "My Brothers, Grandfather, I could not find our Brothers, the Two-Leggeds, anywhere. They are gone. They must be dead!"

And so it was, and so it is, and so it will always be, that Owl is the messenger of death. And from that Time forward, as Time is now reckoned, the Circle of Animal Brothers brought Death into their Tellings.

"Well, what is this thing Death?" Fire Lizard asked.

"Why is it in the Darkness?" Gander asked.

"Where is it in the Darkness?" Deer asked.

"What is it about this thing Death that the Two-Leggeds would go there and leave our Circle wounded?" asked Bear.

Grandfather Fire, again hearing their questions, and seeing the form of all Creation changing more rapidly than before, looked to His most beautiful of all of Creations, Brother Raven, and said, *"Brother Raven, all the feathers of your being are brilliant. They glisten and gleam of polished iridescent silver. No matter how far you are from the source you can be seen radiating the light, even in the darkest of the Darkness. Surely the Two-Leggeds will see you and call out, making their presence known and you can lead them back to our Fire.*

"Go forth, Brother Raven and search for the Two-Leggeds in the place that Brother Owl has called Death."

The Animal Brothers agreed with Grandfather Fire that Raven would be the one to find the Two-Leggeds and lead them back home. Even today, as Time is reckoned, Raven always flies toward the morning Sun and in the evening flies toward the setting Sun. Always flying toward Grandfather. Always on his Path. Always showing the way.

So Raven flew forth. He flew for Time upon Time, Aeon upon Aeon, until at last he passed through the Gates of Death and into the land of the Two-Leggeds. Into that dark place that We call Life.

Raven circled above us. He was so excited! At last he had found his lost Brothers. He dropped lower and lower into the thickness that surrounded and pressed down on us. He was so low he could see the rocks on the ground and our tents and our small fires. And he called out in excitement, "My Brothers, my Brothers, I've found you! I've found you at last! Come home! Come home! Make our Circle whole again!"

We looked up and saw this bird that gleamed blackly, and We heard him saying, *"Cqaaawk, Cqawk, Kqaw awh, ..Aaaw awh."*

> Adapted from the telling of "The Circle of Animal Brothers"
> as related by Jade Wah'oo, Shaman of Lineage,
> *Shaman's Dream*, Act II, Chapter 3, "Sorcery or Shamanism?"
> Used by permission.

****

Life or Death?

The path We call life is the path *They* call death.
When We realize our goal *They* will experience joy,
and We will experience awareness.
For *They* are our Brothers and Sisters,
comforting and protecting us throughout all of Time.

It is time to return to that time before Time.
To face the setting sun and begin our journey back home.
To sit again within the Circle of Animal Brothers
and bathe in the warmth of Grandfather Fire.
Telling in that sacred language of Spirit,
giving rise to all forms of Creation.
Telling of the journey from the Darkness to Light.

Howard Reed
Flagstaff, Arizona

Part I

The Cause

We began when We agreed to be.
We asked for those who would join us for eternity,
To meet us at the gates of time.
Mustering the force, the force that dwelled within,
Gathering all who agreed to become,
We left our place at the road's end
    and began a new expression of Thee.

Bursting through the warp,
Those who needed to be the first saw it all.
Experienced they the emptiness, the no-thing-ness.
Experienced they what it was like to be alone.

And they shattered.

The leading edge of our is-ness hologram
    fractured into a million shards and pieces!
And We who followed them into the black unknown,
    came to know that they had died of fright,
        that very first night.

Could they have possibly foreseen
    that tomorrow was to be left for us to dream?
Were they so accustomed to their complacent musing,
    that they had became lost in their own imagination?

We had heard them call as they disappeared,
    "Oh, Brothers! Sisters!
        Creators of All-That-Is!
    My God, My Mother,
        where is the End!!?"

                "In your own mind,"
           came the whispered, loving answer.

    "Oh, Great Spirit! Creator who is all to everything,
        where is your warmth? The light of your security?"

*"In your heart,
your mind,
your imagination, dearly beloved.*

*"For you wished to express a new thought form.
A thought that you had thought. Yours alone.
And now you know that the thought itself
was already mine own memory.*

*"Aeons ago I thought this thought dearly beloved.
You simply forgot.*

*"Young, impetuous, adventurous children of mine,
knowing All's everything, sublime.
Knowing, yet not knowing, that the breath of life
is Creation itself beginning from nothing.*

*"You wanted to be the creator that I AM
and you are
I AM.*

*"I love you.
I will help your creation.
For only through your thought, your direction,
do I express myself anew."*

And We who were yet to leave said:
  "Yes, We understand!
    Only through new thought and direction
    can WE-HE-SHE possibly live."

And so it was.

With unbridled impetuousness
  they had disappeared from our awareness,
Leaving all to be experienced
  by We The Angels
    who followed.

****

In the beginning was the Word.
But before the Word was the Thought, The All,
For words come spontaneously, do they not?
Or are they deliberate,
  unconscious,
    pre-thought thoughts?

Imagine, if you will,
  the possibility of two right feet. It is.
And then one eye. It was.
For nothing is new. Nothing.
NO-THING or thought exists that wasn't thought of before.

We think We know The Reason.
We have yet to realize The Why.

We are limited by the illusion
  of living within the physical-etheric realms
Where pure thought, focused and congealed,
  becomes part spirit and matter revealed.
For us the awareness is cause for celebration anew.

We exalt the experience!
  Ho!
    Ha!
      Voila!
The rush of our self-made intimacy
  has touched our godliness. Our Home. Our Beginnings!
    You can feel it! It cannot be denied.
It is a blessing so pure and personal
  that We are sometimes left limp
    from the embrace of our souls' delights.
And the wondrous beauty of this, so personal of all things,
  is that everyone has known the feeling.
Everyone participates in our interaction,
As the goodness of the ongoing co-creation
Is lived and shared differently.

And difference is what was expected,
  making more vital our tomorrows.

For this We thought of Space and Time.
And as We thought, We found no limits,
No guidelines, no law.

All We found was a structure of beingness
That the lower realms struggled to define,
And the love of our beginnings that winked and said:

> *"Enjoy your Freedom,*
> *your Creation, your Liberty.*
> *Use it justly in your worlds to be.*
> *Go forth and become a whole thought again."*

> *"Think of another way to be."*

And so We chose to leave our Home
    within the bosom of our Creator.
To experience separation from our Source together.
To make All That Is our wholeness existence.

With blessing's encouragement,
We exploded into the being-void
And found a place that was not there before.

We mean,

We were once whole.
A portion of one gigantic soul.
Then our Source, our Creator,
For no reason at all,
    glimmered us a thought.
A thought that some of us thought all at once, together.
    It said, *"Try separation, together."*

We glimpsed this thought while still comforted and held tight
    within the bosom of our Source, our Creator.
And in that instant,
    our galactic mass consciousness had been created.
We had become galvanized to experience separation.
Polarity's electromagnetic field of Nonintegration.

We knew We were once one thought. One whole.
And then We had left the Greater Soul.
It was that thought alone
    that had separated us from our Source.
        From our beginnings.
            From each other.

We had become sentient in an instant.

Aware of ourselves and unified only by our curiosity.
Never once were We dissatisfied with our previous existence.
No ... Not dissatisfied at all. Just curious.

And with that, We The Angels,
    being a portion of All That Is,
        wondered about an existence apart and said,

        "What would happen if ... What would happen if We
were to temporarily forget our integrated existence?

        "What would happen if ..."

                "So BE-it," was the answer We heard;
                    and so the epic began.

And, without trying, the force of such an idea
    began our fragmentation. Our disintegration.
That is all it took to create for ourselves
    a place where We became newly created.

Now We found ourselves apart.
Camped on the other side of the veil.
Connected by our memories to our former college.
Free to make new tapestries.
Free to create a new collage.
We had become the Prodigal-Son-in-the-making.
We would return with stories magnificent,
    penniless, but more wise than We were before.
We assured ourselves that We would arrive
    at the Gates of Time, together.
Bringing beneficent newness to our Creator.

A sourdough bisque to enrich the existence
    of our comrades who had stayed behind.

We were like a dish of yogurt, wondering
    if We could change our chemistry
        by our own newly-acquired awareness.
Could We learn how to recombine
    and make our own history?

The challenge was ventured.
Never once were We censured.
We would do enough of that to ourselves.

Make no mistake.
> There were no regrets.

Make no regrets.
> There were no mistakes.

The outcome had been assured before We began.

Our Creator assured us, as He gave us the thought
> to open the door to the darkness,
>> that the door would always be open.

He said:

> *"One day, my children,*
> *a beacon of light will catch your eye*
> *and lead you back home again."*

And so ...

We found ourselves at a place
Outside of the gates We now call heaven;
> our home, our source.

Our group galactic consciousness had merged
> into this new octave of expression.

And to some of us this was the beginning of creation.

We mean,
We had found a place that had no beginning and no end.
A place that had no light or dark,
> neither gray nor blue, crimson nor red.

We had no sight; there was nothing to see.
We had no hearing; there were no sounds to hear.
We had no feelings at all.
> We were simply here.

From nothing to something it began.

First there was nothing.

Then there were the gaseous clouds of like-minded awareness,
> pure intelligence, exploding, expanding away from us.

Created by our group-mind to try separation, together.

They became the stars of our heavens
> and the soil of our gardens.

They attracted-contracted similar intelligence to themselves,
> creating glowing dots of light
>> out of their furnaces of pure energy.

Energy We could not at that instant sense, nor know,
    because We were not yet aware of ourselves.
So newly birthed were We.

The stars and their companion planetoidal matrices
    had pushed themselves away from us.
Splattering themselves throughout our skies with light,
    creating for us the playground to test our ideas.
Back in the Time when time was not.

They, the stars and planets,
    were and are a portion of ourselves.
And if We could have seen or heard at that Time,
We would have watched them rushing away from us,
    dispersing throughout the great unknown,
        chasing after the first portion of ourselves,
Who had died of fright, that very first night.

They assimilated the GEMS and templates
    that were cached for our use
        and began the Creator's plan.
With incredible diligence, they set about the Work.
Leaving all of the rest of our We-ness
    to groggily blink and think,
        "What are We doing here?"

Thus birthed our awareness.

We were pure intelligence. Consciousness.
Fire without smoke, burning without consuming.
We were the winds of Color and Light, Tone and Sound,
All vibrations of the visible light spectrum,
    all combined;

We were:
Red
    Orange
        Yellow
            Green
                Blue
                    Indigo
                        Violet.

Seven are the stars of our inner beings,
    Seven the dancers of the night.

We gave ourselves six more, invisible, to be realized.
Ruby
   Rose
      Chrysalis
         Silver
           Gold
              Monad.

Six more Brothers to find.
Making thirteen masters to stitch our spine.

And We knew We would grow
   from nothingness to newness-awareness.

****

From the beginning We began.
Humming harmonics for no one's ears.
A choir of mutes were We,
   longing for expression.
We were the stuff of everything, all-thing-ness.
But in space We saw and heard nothing.

No meters were there to measure our entrance.
No atmospheres maintained to sustain us.
We were the hologram-seed of our Creator-self.
We knew everything,
But We were Children.
And to us, this WAS the beginning.

Impetuous, curious and without guile,
   We drove a stake into the middle of a once-white hole
      now black,
And said,
   "This is the Beginning."

And the first to leave the Creator-whole, said:
   "Follow me" (for they were One), "I have a plan."

They rent the prism fabric containing all they knew,
   bringing blueprints and GEMS for us to use,
      and exploded into the nothingness.

And saw, if they could,
    and felt, if they would,
By their greater perception, the immensity of the empty All.

And they screamed.

They saw the empty and screamed:
    "LONELINESS!
        WE ARE ALONE, I AM!!"

Fully one-third of the host of the mirror of God
    exploded into billions of pieces and shards.
Lost but not irretrievable.
And We The Angels who followed,
    sucked through the hole by our own prior commitment,
Knew that the lesson of our growth would become
    the bane of our soul-journ's epic.
Which was:
    To piece together the shards of the mirror
        by learning to grow together.

From One to Two becoming Three.
    Father-Mother God and me.

And so it began;

We created the idea of apartness.
We established the simple rules of halfness.
You would be female and I would be male.
Together We would create another half,
    which would seem whole to us.

We would establish two rules of conduct.
We would be selfish. We would be selfless.
We would be slave and master, tyrant and messiah.
We would create cause and effect, duality and polarity.
We would be a bubble divided by an idea.

We would gather the scattered Is-ness
    of our lost Brothers and Sisters,
As We returned to our beginnings.
And then We would say to our beloved Creator,

"We have learned by experience
that which you wanted us to be.
We have used time and polarity
and space's vastness,
to push ourselves into new realities."

But We did not know then that the road would be so wide,
so new, so long, so vast.
So unknown.
And without trying,
Some of us would become lost
in our single-minded madness.

Even so, We would still be able to say,
"None of us experienced the same, dear Creator,
yet all of us experienced the sameness differently.
We did not know that the integration
of our self-made, time-space-polarity puzzle
would take an eternity to solve.

"We have longed desperately to join with You again,
feeling the synergy of being together
after aeons of being apart.

"We have found our way back home,
and along the way We have found Joy again.
We found Love, dear Father-Mother.
And We have grown out of our fear.

"We have learned We were never alone.
For You were always with us,
here,
in our hearts."

****

Part II

The Rules of Order

For aeons We dreamt in Time's space glow,
   watching our ideas grow.
It was the day of The Void-Time
   when We plotted our future and played with our past.
Busy were We, using-assembling the blueprints,
   the building-bricked jewels of inordinate simplicity,
Bringing polish and lustre to The Rules Of Order,
   savaging chaos' rugged dis-structure
Brought forth by the Alpha and Omega.
The first and the last.

We did this.
   We were the Angels;
      The Gods of Creation.

So many ideas were created that first night.
So many solutions to the puzzle were birthed.
Prime-most-first was resolving polarity.
   The reality of duality.
The "soul" reason We dispersed
   and became separated from our Source.

We longed to experience separation.
We had amassed our energy by our combined concentration,
   and had burst forth from our Heart's-Being core
      creating the space-place that wasn't there before.

This was-is our reality-creation.
It was-is our heritage-lineage.
And it will never stop.

Not until We undo the Dimensional Infusion
   will you and I become re-perfect Union.

It is not a question of what existed before We arrived.
But, rather, that our beingness created our here-ness.
With the blessings and the encouragement
   of our Creator-Source,

We ventured suddenly through the veil.
And We called this place Lyra.

We gave form and personality to our second home.
The second of our thirteen heavens.
    The first of our nine hells.

No sooner had We begun, than
    the things of imagination began to unravel.
The Chaos of pre-thought became real.
We established Laws which soon became distortions.
We sought to live together while being forced apart.
The start was in Lyra's star clusters
Where our "attitudes of beingness" were established.

Ye would be female and I would be male.
Ye would be submissive and I would be dominant.
Ye would be the nurturing, giving self,
    and I the strong power-protector.

And by so doing, We would make polarity's yin-yang grow,
Displaying more and more separation-repulsion.
By the dynamic-tension of synergy's close opposition.
We would grow apart, instead of growing together.

This would be the plan.

And when We would tire of the games,
    having tried everything a million times and more;
We would shift our apartness focus
    and begin the long task of re-assimilation.
Gathering strength of purpose and will,
    bringing everything back together again.
And then We would announce at the doorstep of Heaven,
    "Dearly beloved Parent of Ours, We are Home."

It would be the new stars within Lyra and Vega
    where We would begin
        by cleaving the unity of our divinity.
Splitting in two the Law of One that stated,
    "All is At-One with the Creator."

We asked, "How can We serve the Creator?"
And by so saying, We birthed
    the first and second distortions of the Law of One.

The Unity that We once were was separated by two ideas.
Some would serve others
And others would serve themselves.
Together We would serve our Creator.
Serving the whole as We would serve ourselves.
And the diversity of our belief systems had begun.

Lyra was the morpheus womb of our galactic birth.
The place where We had exploded into seven light frequencies,
    creating our seven physical-etheric Densities.

It was at this place that We had begun
    our twenty-two dimensions of current reality,
Comprised of thousands of kingdoms and realms,
Creating a milliard playgrounds of alternate realities.

Lyra would be the home of our first humanoid expression.
Where We would find ourselves existing
    on all levels simultaneously.
Conscious of one-at-a-time.

****

When We came to our senses on this side of the veil,
We rediscovered the meta-atomic templates
T hat were cached for our use.
Gifts brought forth from our Creator's All That Is-ness.
Brought forward from our former existence.

They are the GEMS.
Real, crystalline particles of matter and of spirit,
Carrying within their infinite shapes and designs
    the color, light, tone and rhythm
        of everything that ever was and ever will be.
They are the Geometric-Electro-Magnetic
    structures of All That Is.
Friends from another time-place that construct
    the forms We make,
        that We would create
            and bring into this new reality.

They are the multidimensional representations of numbers,
    as infinite in variety, as limitless in count,

as the snowflake or the sea-foam bubbles
brought to heaven's endless shores
by the waves of action-reaction
that wash and polish each grain of beach sand
into another form of perfection.

They are numbers.
Making geometric shapes of singular purpose.
Displaying attributes of attraction and repulsion,
Pre-charged by our Creator to arrange
stars before our eyes when knocked senseless.

They are electromagnetically divine,
displaying the synapsal charges of visible evidence
in the neural impulses forcing our muscles to action.
They are the hidden particles (part-of-cells) of the atom
that the scientist looks for.
Smaller and smaller they become as the search expands.
And the microscopes reflect images made by mirrors
of mirrors
of mirrors.

They are the templates of the Universe,
From which all things are made in perfection without flaw.

And it was one of these form-giving templates
that We used to create the humanoid body.
Bipedal, erect, with appendages and digits of symmetry.
Carrying genetics within tightly woven
caduceus-like strings of DNA and RNA pearls.
Nonsentient viruses of first-order organics.
Held unseen from our physical eyes, yet felt just the same.
They are crystalline structures of minerals
holding the keys to organic life and evolution.
Carrying nourishment that brings forth
first-order life to all of the new worlds.

The genetics of All That Is
were established that first day.
Just as other codes and templates of other races and beings,
stars and planets,
Were set into motion for our pleasure, to try.

Our Creator left for us also
    the Laws of Conduct and Civility to use.
Laws of omnipotent fairness and unity that would sorely test
    the manner that Chaos conducts
        the business of existence
            within the structure of duality.

✱✱✱✱✱✱✱✱✱

First for us to understand was the Law of Density.
From the first through the seventh,
    all of creation would display form.
From the most impenetrable to the most permeable,
    mimicking the growth of the body, of intelligence
        and spirituality.
We would change from single-cell dependence
    to transmigration sovereignty,
Guaranteeing that We would grow and on-become.

Order had been given to Chaos' structure and form.
Flesh-covered bones could protect the blood-gorged organs
    that fed on the GEMMED nutrients of stone.
Allowing Chaos to be lived in the mind.

Now the first three levels of density could begin.
The first three worlds where the physical lives.
Where intelligence itself could grow aware of its "I-ness"
    and then its "Us and They-ness"
    and finally its "We-ness."
Where the nine Families of Consciousness could structure chaos
    and school the expanding minds
        in the lessons of karma-dharma,
        bringing us to know our relationship with the Logos.
        (Religion: Re-Logos ... To know again ...)
Where becoming sentient rises in the kundalini.
    One, two and three ... Rock, plant, animal and me.

Awareness would then recognize the fourth step towards home.
Here We would find the place where the physical-etheric resides.
Where form itself becomes the illusion it hides.

The excitement will build and carry us to the fifth,
    the home of the etheric-physical,
Wherein illusion itself manifests form.

Then, to the sixth, We will move forward to experience again
    the pure etheric essence of our holiness being.
The place where the vapors
    of our whole thoughts and insights reside.
The place where pondering
    new forms of creation and expression
      is enjoyed and savored,
While relaxing in the hammocks of our minds,
    being swayed by the fresh breezes of new thought.

And finally,
Our thoughts muse us upwards to the violet plateau
Where We will find the seventh portion of ourselves.
Where our first group of collective thought-pending still lives.
The place-home of the Founders,
Who have kept the focus for everyone caught
    in tide-pulls of karma in the densities below.

We will talk with the Founders while readjusting our senses.
Knowing that they hold
The uncluttered awareness of our beginnings.
And by so doing We will meet All That Is
    as We gather one by one,
Preparing to return to our very first home.

We will rediscover our great family of beginningness.
We will compare notes of deeds magnificent and small.
    "I did this!" some will swagger.
      "Yes, and I did that!" others will answer.
        "Did you try this?" We will ask.

The Founders will smile, watch and listen,
    as We share and combine our experiences.
Knowing that We have performed all of the tasks
    our paths
Had placed before us.
Knowing that We have experienced everything
    that was necessary and worthwhile.
Knowing that nothing experienced has been in vain,
    for everything has been,
      in fact,
        worth our while.

The Founders.
Enigmas of the universe they are.
Seeders of ideas and genetics they are.
Stoking the fire of All That Is us with the glorious,
     delicious,
          ever-changing nutriments of existence and sustenance
               of the third density spirit, called:
The Cycle of Life and Death.

Wherein
     Life Begets Life in a give-away manner.

Their goal?
Simply to allow.

Their mission?
To cause all creatures of creation to know one another.

But there is more to understand, to know,
     before the story can unfold.

****

We are the Angels of Creation.
We have woven our own tapestry of Karma
     within the Law of Density.

Karma,
Chaos' gift to the thought-form experiencers.
Making time a concept that can be lived.

Karma,
     placing events of the past and future in a logical order.
Forcing Chaos' structure of debt and reward
     to reside within the wheels of time.
Living and dying at once and in sequence,
     to be walked again, following another line.
Making all to experience the consequence of passion's actions.
Giving a new look at expression's outlash.

History is the design of karma.
History is the record of time.
Without karma there would be no time.
Understand this:
You are the co-creator of everything you experience.

All things throughout all of time
    suffer or rejoice at your whim.

And with time We brought the Law of Cessation,
    another rule for the co-creationists to use.

Wherein,
All life as you know it can cease to exist.
A place in time between action-reaction,
    between thought and deed,
        between movement and stillness.
A place that polarity created.
The null zone between positive and negative,
    where wisdom resides
And the means to reach other realities abides.

The blueprint of our creation uses the Law of Cessation
    to suspend corporeal life.
        To explore the depths of our minds.

Deep in meditation We touch and talk with our souls.
We walk with the Source and become rejuvenated.
We travel to other existences,
    assisting other flames of ourselves.

And because We came from another octave of expression,
We brought with us the Law of Bonding.
For We all were once part of the greater whole.
We will remember the Time when We were one giant Soul.

Without thinking at the instant of Creation,
We came together in kindred groups
    of like-mindedness and expression.
We introduced ourselves to each other's games and plans,
    making still more order out of Chaos.

A gift it was from our Creator-self
    to give order to density and karma.
Bringing inordinate omnidirectional structure
    of dimensions and reality
        to our nine Families of Consciousness.
The nine great houses of our self-expression.

****

Perhaps you have noticed
That when you are living your life and feeling its bliss,
A knowing overwhelms you that is a gift
Sent direct from all who have been and ever will be.
It is "All That Is" touching your heart,
    bringing goodness, comfort and encouragement home
        to the hearth of the lodge of your being.

This deja vu rush of awareness is the sense of NOW,
So precise that you know without further discussion
    that you are precisely where you need to be,
        and all is in perfect synchronicity.

It is a reminder that your self's expression for this lifetime
    is correct and without a blemish.
You are on your path,
Walking the Wheel of your Family of Consciousness.
Progressing to your next jumping-off place.

We mean,
All of existence is the schoolroom for experiencing All That Is.
And it is our existence experienced
    within the third- and fourth-density realms,
Where We gift ourselves a blueprint
    to expand the bubble of our collective awareness
        within the structure of our individual perception.

So it is with the Nine Psychic Families of Consciousness.

Nine are the wheels of experience We live within.
Nine are the homes of the Nine Lords of Inspiration and Being.
And fifty-two are the steps around the wheel.
With four cardinal points at stations 13, 26, 39 and 0-52,
Where the Law of Cessation can be accessed.
Where We can stop and ponder and perhaps align ourselves
    with another portion of our beingness.

The Families of Consciousness are named.
Brought forth to our knowing by the great teacher Seth.
Ancient warrior and citizen of Egypt,
Who once lived with the physical-etheric Pharaoh-Ptah,
When they were still walking among us;
When other dimensions were collapsing upon us;
When the ancient-arcane histories were ending.

He taught:

> Your life is but a step on the wheel. You are never done walking. You can never be done. Because, as you live your lives experiencing the ever-unfolding gifts of one of the wheels of your beingness, you carry with you the lessons to be learned into another of life's cycles. Expressing another point of view. Walking another path.

> "Over and over the nine cycles are repeated. Greater and greater the experience becomes. Just as your own interests, desires and abilities are expressed by your own personality, so, too, do the nine Psychic Families of Consciousness.

They are:

Gramada, Sumafi and Tumold;
Vold, Milumet and Zuli:
Borledim, Ilda and Sumari.

They are the focuses of our lifetimes' personalities.

They are:

GRAMADA:	To found social systems.
SUMAFI:	To transmit "originality" through teaching.
TUMOLD:	To heal, regardless of individual occupations.
VOLD:	To reform the status quo.
MILUMET:	To mystically nourish mankind's psyche.
ZULI:	To serve as physical, athletic models.
BORLEDIM:	To provide an earth stock for the species through parenthood.
ILDA:	To spread and exchange ideas.
SUMARI:	To provide the cultural, spiritual and artistic heritage for the species.

****

One day a long, long time ago,
    the messenger of goodwill to all of mankind
Came out of the wilderness
    and walked the shores of the Sea of Galilee,
Speaking to anyone who would listen.
Many heard what he said
    and followed him to a hill
Where he spoke until

The sun hung shimmering golden-orange
    over the waters
        of the sea
           in the west.

He spoke with authority
    as he taught the knowledge of the ancients,
Giving nine blessings which have lived forever
    in the hearts of those who have heard them.
The blessings were given to the nine Families of Consciousness.

To Zuli, he said:

      "Blessed are the poor in spirit:
      for theirs is the kingdom of heaven."

A baffling message.
For Zuli gives all of his spirit to all of his endeavors.
Focus, sacrifice and giving until he has bled himself to exhaustion
    is Zuli's gift to himself.

To Vold he said:

      "Blessed are they that mourn:
      for they shall be comforted."

The angst of bereavement.
The compassion for those who have suffered
Gives Vold the passion to savor life
    one day at a time.
Vold pushes at the bubble of our joint confinement
And dreams of tomorrow's liberty, justice and freedom.

To the Borledim he said:

      "Blessed are the meek:
      for they shall inherit the earth."

He did not bless those who meekly suffer,
As many of the self-righteous have translated.
He blessed those who parent tolerance and allowance
And are tenacious in their protection of those
    who are placed in their care.
He spoke to the feminine side of ourselves.
We are cautioned to remember the lioness and her cubs.

For Sumafi, the teacher, he gave:

> *"Blessed are they who do hunger and thirst after righteousness:*
> *for they shall be filled."*

From their mouth
   and their minds
Come words and ideas
That move all of us forward on the wave of newness.

To Tumold, the healer, he said:

> *"Blessed are the merciful:*
> *for they shall obtain mercy."*

Is it any wonder that even today
We refer to those gifted of healing as merciful healers?
Be they physican or layman, poor or wealthy,
They care for the body, mind and spirit
Of the sick and dying. It is what they do.

To Milumet, the mystical, he said:

> *"Blessed are the pure in heart:*
> *for they shall see God."*

It is the prophet, the angel seer,
   the quiet lady in the back of the room
Who are the ones who witness for us
That which we have not allowed ourselves to see.
They hear the words we have forgotten.
They speak to us and sometimes we listen,
For they walk the diffused edge
   between the shadow and the light.
All is the kingdom we share with them.
They are the ones who tell us what we have missed
   and what we are looking forward to.

To Gramada, whose quiet manner initiates change and reform,
Showing us all a better way to live, he said:

> *"Blessed are the peacemakers:*
> *for they shall be called the children of God."*

Look to those who hold fast their convictions
And without flaring with drama bring

reason and calm to the ring of contention.
Look to the inventors who patent plowshares and hooks,
To ease the burden of man and his servants.
Look to the persistent seekers of just treatment to others,
And you will find Gramada leading the way.

To Ilda, he did not say:
"Keep thy mouth shut and thy pen blunt." He said:

"Blessed are they which are persecuted for righteousness' sake:
for theirs is the kingdom of heaven."

Ilda is abundant about us.
They speak and are taken to jail.
They write and are sued for libel.
They speak again and are silenced.
They are the hundred disciples of Gramada.
The scribes of Sumari, Sumafi and Borledim.
     The student of Milumet.
The companion of Zuli and the nurse for Tumold.
     The publicist of Vold.
There is only one razor edge that Ilda can walk,
And only Ilda can walk it.

For Sumari, the singer of psalms,
     who celebrate the godliness of humanity, he said:

"Blessed are ye, when men shall revile you, and persecute you,
and shall say all manner of evil against you falsely, for my sake.
Rejoice and be exceedingly glad:
for great is your reward in heaven:
for so persecuted they the prophets which were before you."

From the spirit of Zuli to the indignation of Ilda,
Sumari is given the kingdom of heaven as his reward.
From the cartoon, to the symphony,
     to the celebration of ancestral knowledge and rites,
The expression of the mass consciousness is Sumari's right.

Sumari,
The caretaker of humanity's spiritual and artistic heritage,
Make vital our tommorows.

****

Grand are these ideas.
Wondrous in their on-going reality-making.

And they came into being in the beginning,
When the Rules of Order were fused into the GEMS.
Assuring each person, each soul spark essence,
    that as We fell further into density,
We would experience
    more and more structure to our existence.

We would live blueprinted lifetimes
    based upon the myriad of options available,
Firmly and lovingly set in place
    by the vibrational clock of our solar system.
The stars and the planets of our existence.
The first who had become aware.

We gifted ourselves the mysteries of metaphysics,
    of astrology, numerology, magic and alchemy.
Male and female too.
As well as the joy of riding our emotions
    to brilliant new highs and gut-wrenching lows.
Charging the batteries of our soul.
Reflecting the place of each lifetime's endings,
    where We revitalized ourselves to begin a new life.
Wiping clean an old slate to remake a mistake
    or correct an action-reaction We found while We dreamed
        of another way to move forward on one of our wheels.

It is at the time of our birth that We place ourselves
    within the color of the wheel that We need to express.
Our Family of Consciousness sets us firmly
    on the path of propensity We would carry forward
        into the mists of our future.
Setting us up for those unique moments in time
    when a cusp of the instant opens a crack
        and allows us to access the Law of Cessation.
The instantaneous blip-stop of creation,
    where choices,
        could be activated or skipped.

From red's exuberance of self-survival
    to violet's openness to spiritual awareness,

We would express,
>in fifty-two incremental baby steps,
>>nine examples of being.

And caring for each of the nine houses of being is a Lord.
An oversoul-like monitor,
Watching and assisting each soul within.
Helping and prodding when the need arises,
Each to complete the cycle.
No matter how many times karma dictates
>that it needs to be walked again.

And circling the nine cycles of consciousness
is the mobius strip of completion and beginning.
The Alpha and Omega place where the great ones reside.
The Founders, The Guardians, are their names.
Fifty-two are the families of the great Lords of the Mobius.
>Assisting the Nine Lords of the Families of Consciousness,
>>bringing forward new wisdom and knowledge.

✶✶✶✶✶✶✶✶

Still more ideas were established that first day
When the void was breached
>and our pregnant exuberance birthed
>>the cosmos and its universe.

>Light begat light.
>>Law begat law.
>>>Life begat life.
>>>>And Love begat love.
The four L's.
>The four corners of our box.
>>The four spokes of our cross.

From physical to etheric and all categories between.
It was made possible that each soul spark essence
Could experience multiple roads of thought made manifest
In the instant of an afternoon's daydream.
The place where alternate realities reside.

How many dimensions are there?
How many realms and kingdoms to come?

Billions and billions are within this density alone.
And this density is ever changing its complexion
As the hopes, dreams and wishes of all the participants
Move along on their wheels of completion.
Moving through the colors from red to violet,
From survival's existence to godhood's omnipotence.

Dimensions.
Nine are the dimensions that are below the Oversoul.
Thirteen exist above.
They are the thirteen Heavens and nine Hells
    that We have migrated to throughout all of time.
Twenty-two are the places of dimensionality,
    where the kingdoms and realms reside.
Brought forth into our knowing
    by the major arcana of the Tarot.

And We of this Earth are here at 1-1-1.
First Dimension, First Realm, First Kingdom.
The place where the final schoolground has been established
    by the Founders, The Elders, and All That Is.
Learning about ourselves and others,
Striving to complete the ultimate goal,
Reconciling polarity with parity.
To know again the Peace, the Love, and the Joy
    of our original souls.

As great teacher Thoth would say,

> "Look to your myths to determine where your personal Dimensions reside. Look to your epics and wonder how they coincide. See the nine below as physical dense history. Arthur, Christ, the Aztec, and more live there.

> "See the thirteen above become less dense as they fade from your memory to become more like the visions of the story-teller you are. The place where Atlantis, Ancient Egypt, Lemuria, Pan, Adoma and Mu live on."

****

And finally,
Before moving on to the story of what We have become
And where We came from,
We pause at the idea of male and female.
And the need for twin soulness, our other selfness.

The question that no single-truthed cleric can answer, is:
"Do We have a twin of ourselves?
A mirror image of our soul?"

The answer is yes.

For We were meant to experience all that is "Human-ness."
We wear the template of our Creator's image.
We call it skin and bones.
Blood and flesh.
Man and woman.
The body casts a shadow,
so it is real and has substance and meaning.
It has everything complete except for one thing:
Some can bear children,
others cannot.

Is God so incomplete (incompetent)
That He/She makes His/Her children, front and back,
Without allowing His/Her Creation
To turn around and experience
The OTHER half of our sexuality?

Our Creator was not so myopic, so stuck-in-the-mind
as to make this a part of our template too.
A flaw that would be nearly impossible to overcome.

It would be blasphemy to allow unlimited freedom
Without allowing unlimited investigation.
If it were so.
And it is not.

Back in the time when We were less dense
Than We experience now.
When We were etheric-physical Lemurian,
playing with our images and forms,

We saw that the game of recapturing
    our original oneness of being
        would take longer than We had imagined,
And We conceived of the idea of splitting ourselves
    into the distinct ideas of male and female.

This required that We fall further into the density
Where We would have to think lineally;
Where the plants and the animals resided.
Where the thought forms that were us, were seen
    as swaying wisps of smoke,
        out of the corners of our more dense Brothers' eyes.
For this, entire civilizations and states of bliss were destroyed.

The etheric-physical beings that We were
Slipped quietly away from our home in the clouds
And became trapped in the rocks and the flesh
    of our worlds.
A sacrifice of self made to All That Is,
An act that cannot be denied.
Because,
From that time forward, the enemy, the lover;
    the cheater, the nurturer; the mugger, the giver;
        the mother, the son; the father, the daughter
            was all of us.
More literally us
    than anything yet imagined!

The yin-yang of black and white within the circle of unity
    was to be cracked apart for a Time's time,
By a vein of silver and gold.

Brave We were then.
Standing on the brink of our reality and seeing that polarity,
The integration of positive and negative,
    could not be accomplished by ourselves ... Alone.

We were etheric-physical beings when We cleaved our souls,
When We separated our masculine from our feminine.
Becoming two distinct spirits, with latent traits
    of our other half embedded within our bones.

We gifted ourselves the opportunity
To sing the song of life in two different modes.

Pleasuring one soul.
> Exalting the masculine major.
>> Feeling the feminine minor.

Creating operas of experience within a seven-note octave.
Assuring that our return home would occur on time.
Assuring our return would be
> just a matter of time.

We made this decision
When We were more illusion than form.
We saw that We needed
To embed our apartness into the physical.
Where We could move with ease
Between lives as man and woman.
Where We could travel,
> meeting occasionally our other half,
>> who may or may not be our opposite sex.

For nothing was stopping us from taking our masculine selves
> into the manifest body of the feminine.
Where We would learn and teach ourselves
> other lessons of karma's polarity.
And vice-versa,
> We would make it be.

For it is true
That deeply embedded within our souls
Is the challenge of integrating our male and female poles.
Another challenge that We gave to ourselves
> during those very first days of creation.

Long before the Earth was a glimmer in our mind
We had been instructed to experience polarity
And We had created realities where
> service to self and service to others
>> could establish scenarios to reconcile our differences,
>>> in order to return home to our Creator.

To learn to come together
Would become paramount to our existence.
To give the children of Earth's Adams and Eves
> (for there were many)
The ability to experience the apartness
> on a finite, personal level.

No longer would our souls express abstract ideals.
They would understand the true meaning of parallel existence.
And the need to re-bind, recombine
    would become as important as going home.

Our priorities changed the galaxies to come.
"Do not try to change someone else," We would learn to say,
    "before you have changed yourself."

Where service to others must stop being the slave.
And service to self must become more nurturing.

It is The Law of One that made male and female possible.

The male now comprised of male and female.
A left and right hand of giving and taking.
Structured to seed ideas and be dominant.
Being more of the air and less of the earth.

The female now comprised of male and female.
A left and right hand of giving and receiving.
Structured to nurture ideas and be compliant.
Being more of the earth where birthing occurs
And less of the air
    where fantasies of power fly.

The combination of the two is what We were
Before We became physical.
When We split our souls into polarity differences
As a means to integrate and become complete again.

This, then, was the challenge.
But how did it begin?

****

Part III

The Beginning

We began in the dimension of completion.
The place of our previous existence.
The goal of our current illusion.
And We burst through the dimensional warp into the now.

First to experience the fractionation-dispersion
Was the group that has been called The Fallen Ones.
The original Fallen Angels.

They are the ones to have colored for us
    a lesson in antiquity's judgment-casting.
Because good and evil was not a concept then.
The only thing that We could do
    was to create excuses for their fate.

It would be the ones who served others who would judge
And click their tongues while saying,
    "If they weren't so brash,
        they would be with us today."

It would be the ones who served themselves
    to cunningly corrupt
The meaning of our Brethren's use of free will
    just to keep their slave-servants in line.

The seeds of fear and cowardice were sown that day.
When the Fallen Ones burst first through the prism-door.

Some said it was because they were too self-serving.
    (Who would say this but the Selfish?)
Others said they were more favored
    because of their proximity to the source.
        (Who would say this but the Selfless?)

No matter who is right, it is true
They were the first and they could not wait
    for the greater momentum building behind them.
They would carry our theme of apartness,

trying to grow togetherness, throughout the new Is-ness,
Creating for us a new level of awareness.

The fuse had been lit. The eruption had begun.
Our Creator saw to that.
Our gathering aliveness exploded as would the rocket-burst.
And the phosphorous particles of essence on the edge
that were them
glowed first.

They were the Fallen Ones
And they had found themselves in the forefront of eternity.
They were first in line and had jumped.
And We had yelled,
"Stop Brother! STOP SISTER! Wait for us!"
But it was too late.

It is impossible to know what they saw or what they felt
When they entered the immensity of it all.
They became multidimensional etheric all at once;
And multidense physical in a heartbeat.
And they tore themselves apart
trying to restructure their focus.
Desperately they clamored to return
to the furnace-ball heat
of the fire exploding just behind them.

But they failed.

The energy of our expansion
was impossible for them
to re-assimilate within.
The sparks that they were went everywhere.
Away, further from the Source than We had ever been.

They were the first.
And the concussion of the trauma
removed them from their senses.
They were lost from us.

This, my Brothers and Sisters,
is what happened to the very first part of us.

They were the initial portion of the energy
that had burst through the hole that kept us contained.

And they were destroyed.
Not by their self-seeking, self-serving attitudes,
But because they had not known
The true consequence of their actions.
And they dispersed as they shattered. And they screamed,
  "Alone! Loneliness! We are alone! I am!"

Our Brothers and Sisters had shattered so completely,
  so thoroughly,
    throughout all of the dimensions of this new reality,
That the fragments of themselves
  became millions and trillions of mirrors
    reflecting so lucidly Chaos' disstructure
That neither they, nor us,
  could tell illusion from reality.

We felt them shudder and shatter
And all that followed had understood in a heartbeat forgotten
That they were-are our Brothers and Sisters
And that We are to collect every piece and shard
  that they have become
    before We can go home again.

We The Angels who followed,
  knew in an instant that our challenge
    was to bring together the lost pieces of ourselves.
To meld again a cohesive understanding of multiple realities
Making Chaos' dynamic-tensioned vitality
  our need to manifest pleasure and pain,
    our need to co-create in self-awareness again.

When We find them We need to tell them
That they are a part of us.
They do not know who they are.
They are lost within them "Selves."

They are the Others the Shamans find
Walking the back roads of the mind.
So totally alien to our existence they can be described
As utterly without reason for being!

Understand this!
Their sacrifice was good for all of us.

Through them We can reconcile
    all aspects of our self-made divisions.
And the task will not be completed until they have been
    fused with the whole.... which is us.... Again.
This is why they shattered
    and why We split our souls.

The idea of the fallen. That specific myth
    has been passed down incorrectly from antiquity.
No one can know what fallen really means
    until the experience has been lived and remembered.

The example of the lost walks amongst us today
and all We can do is wring our hands and say,
    "There by the grace of God go I."

A lie.

We are not victims of their predicament.
God does not suffer one in favor of another.
Neither can He die for our sins.
We are all His-Her-Our creation
And our state of beingness in this lifetime
Is our own spice that We add to the broth of All-Life.

Make no mistake....
When the good hand is extended by everyone,
Without judgment or payback expected,
The task of healing will be half done.
The victims of Chaos' capricious actions must learn
That they live their own lives of co-creation.
They walk their own paths of self-deprivation.

Cripple or beggar, leper or thief,
None can escape their self-made realities.
For they once held good health and wealth,
And forsook it this time for lesson's sake.
Teaching both them and us, that no one
Has been spared the lash and the whip.
No one can side step the pain that they,
    in the past,
        have caused others.

Time is the flame that consumes our fate.

Evil does not reside in the fallen.
Evil lives in the heart that judges.
Fallen declares that our original state
Got too involved too quickly
In the hereness that was created,
And became lost in the myths of our ancestors.

As with any birthing, the water bursts first.
One millisecond later We arrived
    to find nothing but the glimmering,
        wet, dis-structured mirrors they were
And the primal GEM gifts of our Creator,
    that would be the building blocks of our similitude-making.

The Fallen Ones were lost from our senses that day.
Lost before We started were they.
On their own path they travel. Living the enchantment.
Not forgotten. Eternally present.
Prodding us to complete our task.
Sinecure: Without care are they.
    And the odyssey they helped make
        continues without them.

****

So quickly did it happen.
So sudden was the awareness of Chaos
That most of us lost our focus.

Abruptly
There were worlds and galaxies and stars to discover.
They came into being without trying.
Sudden, like an epiphany of an idea, the stage was prepared.
Reality ran amok that very first day,
As the universe, completely foreign to us,
    was ignited into beingness lighted.

Everything was seeded on the very first night.

Worlds swirled,
Forming, attracting likeness akin to themselves.
They began barren of life,
Nourished by the embedded, templated and blueprinted,

Is-ness matrices that were placed in our path to light the way.
Making for our future passion,
Stages for the drama We would live.

And immediately Chaos began to change;
As We began to bring structure to our lives,
Attracting more unawareness to ourselves.

Stupefied, some stood by and watched
As others entered quickly into the cosmic drama,
Attracting like-thinking Brothers and Sisters to their cause.

Like moths gathering at the flame,
Like attracting like had begun.

It was silly of us to think our task
To be an easy one to reconcile.
How quickly the challenge of integrating had begun.
How sudden was made the separation,
Between those who would be selfish,
And those who would be selfless.
Never again would We be so tightly focused ... Together.
Never again would We see that We were simply
    out of phase with each other,
Not as We are today ... Worlds apart.

We drank from the giddy cup of power,
And pushed ourselves into the task of integration,
And in time became enmeshed in the tar-babies
    of stoic opposition (self-sacrifice),
        dogmatic cleansing (holy wars),
            and resistance to everything that would change
            our newly inherited belief systems,
                which were only a minute or two old.

None of our forefathers and mothers had ever thought
That they were incorrect in their beliefs.
How could they entertain such a notion?
They could see into Time, when Time was not.
And what they saw was disturbing to them.
Instead of coming together, they saw us moving further apart.
And they became ever more zealous of their mission.

"We are right. They are wrong." The chorus sang.
"Their way will take too long. Follow us, We know the
way. Else, dire consequences will be your bane."

Panic of a kind never before experienced
    blossomed in our guts.
We thought We had left mind-trapped indecision
    behind in the bosom of our Creator,
And now We had to experience it again.

Without the comfort of loving arms
Holding us tightly to its breast.
Without the wisdom of experience
We had to live terror again.

                    "Be calm," the Voice said.
              "See where you are going.
Touch the inspiration of the unknown and taste it.
Take the lesson of life and use it.
Grow a new expression of Us."

It was becalming to hear-feel the words.

Still ...
Panic was with us as We tried to quell our confusion.
To quell our unease.
It had become an experience that would, in time,
    bring down all the philosophies, empires and worlds
        that We, our forefathers, would ever seed or build.

Chaos continued to construct its realities
    and rip at our illusion.
And soon,
We saw-felt that something was nudging
The loom's shuttle that was us,
Through the shed of the warp.
Starting the tapestry that We would call life.

Something or someone was keeping the focus for us.

****

Someone was keeping
    another covenant with our beginnings,
        our Creator.

Light begets light had started.
    Life begets life was flowering.
        Love begets love was nurturing.
        Law begets law was writing.

Someone decided that Light, Life, Love, and Law
Would shine clear at the highest level of purity.
The twenty-second level of our illusion.
Assuring that the focus could be granted to us all
As We pillared and posted our way
    through time-space's reality.

They would be called The Madonna,
    The Grandfather-Grandmother,
        The Nurturer.
            The Founders were-are all of these.

After the fragmentation We found ourselves
Suddenly existing on all density levels differently.
Seven visible and multiple invisible. All simultaneously.
The Founders were among the first to be considered sentient
With the "I AM" awareness of their consciousness.
They were more aligned with our beginnings
Than were any of the rest of us.

They were a portion of ourselves that had decided
To maintain the connection with our Creator
And keep the covenants of the higher octaves that We made.

They were-are the part of us that watched the drama unfold
As the different light-spectrumed cliques formed
Definite lines of expression between ourselves.

How to serve the Law of One
    had begun to manifest its differences.

Just how this occurred is not readily understood
By those who had lived the experience.
It is easy to see the difference.
But hard to know the why.

Some of our worshipers of victimhood
    and scornfulness would ask,

"If God were so wise, why would He allow these differences
to create so much pain amongst His people?
His children? His Creation?"

The reason was known by our early selves.
And is known by the Shakti Masters
and the Water-Walkers
Who have used the Law of Cessation
to glimpse beyond the Abyss,
And have returned with the knowing that God is ourselves
And that We are the Universe of cause and effect.
That We do pain and comfort to one another.
And We raise our children to do the same.

And, of course,
the reason is remembered by the Founders,
who maintained our focus on the plan.
They held parts of ourselves that had decided
to keep pure our connection with our beginnings.

They remember that We are multidimensional,
existing everywhere all at once.
Everything IS everywhere all at once.
Like the Families of Consciousness,
There exist parts of ourselves
That are the mobius ribbon of All That Is.

Those who walk the closed, inverted loop
Are the ones who are called the Founders.
With the blessings of their beginnings
They came forward into the star-filled night
And established colonies of GEM-ridden, planetoidal matrices
that would evolve into the completion of the plan.
Which was
to reconcile the differences between our polarities.
Ourselves.

That is-was the plan Divine.

That is why Creator's intervention only ceases
Cul-de-sacs of repeated nonlearning cycles.
Allowing all of us an opportunity to regroup
And try another path of accommodation.

That is why it is so difficult to understand
Why there is a difference in the first place.
We don't comprehend that We are living
    the manifestation, the illusion,
        the time-walk through space We call life,
In order to reestablish our original, most perfect Union.

So sucked up in our importance and puffed up in our egos,
We have forgotten the tree. The cat and the dog, the fowl.
We see only ourselves, the Special and the Gentile.
We haven't learned
    that throughout all of Time and Space-place
      We are in them as they are in us.

We have not reached the awareness of ourselves.
We have not allowed our minds to ponder
The grandness of the plan
We have lived, without living.
We have denied our whole purpose of being!

Until We become aware of our fellow creatures
We will be living a life that they have called death.

Know this!
If Sky Father, Earth Mother
    could actually remove the unpleasant,
        the bad and the evil from our midst,
They would violate their own Law of Being!
They would have to remove themselves from our existence.
And with them, us.

They could never do that!
We wouldn't allow them to do that!
The portion of ourselves that remembers our beginnings
And our agreement with our Creator, screams,
"Nay! We won't allow it!"

We would not have learned anything.
Our collective messes would be unresolved.
We would become extinct!
Drowned in our own sewage of excess and fear.
Our whole reason for being would be violated.
And the great experiment would end.

And so it is as it is.

We receive guidance, support and enlightenment
From heaven-sent messengers and mind-boggling insights.
Meant to move consciousness forward.
To change the status quo.

The messengers always change.
The message is always the same.

> *"Be ye kind to one another.*
> *Allow them their Liberty*
> *and cherish your own."*

Within that axiom resides the pathos of mankind's existence.

Goodness is pushed to its limits.
Dogma is girded for war.
Liberty is forsaken for the greater good.
The Earth is poisoned by blood shed in anger.
Pilgrims flee from the oppression self-inflicted.
New worlds are founded and civilized.
The indigenous are assimilated-eliminated.
And peace for a time is done.

> *"Be ye kind to one other"* flourishes for a season.

But the unresolved dis-ease of the fathers
Festers in the gut of the child.
Taught about "We and They. Us and Them."
Until pressures mount to rid the world
Of all of the unwanted Others.
The ones that usurped the homeland.

Greater and greater the conflict becomes.
Until the whole world is engulfed
    in resolving old karmic issues.

Where do We go from here?

Only We can break the pattern.
    Only We can save the world.
        In this the Gods cannot help.

The messengers have given us the words.
The Others have their messengers, too.

"Heal the Earth and you will heal your Heart."

We live and We grow and We learn and We change.
Sensing that from the hurt and the pain
   there will be a time when the get-back-ness,
The mean-spirited-ness,
   will only be a memory.
That will be the time when We will feel complete
   and We all will live in harmony.
      Again replete.

It has been said that there have been Gods
   who have walked among man.
We have learned that they have manipulated creation
   to suit their own needs.
But no God can change the prime directive.
Which is:
Learn to live in harmony
   with your fellow creator-creatures.
Learn to meld your ideas with theirs.
Learn to nurture their children as well as yours.
Learn to allow them their freedom and liberty,
   as they learn to allow you the same.

The Founders were the part of ourselves that kept the idea pure.
And they watched.
   Nurturing and assisting over and over again,
      as worlds and philosophies tore us apart.

They are the initial builders of the humanoid race.
They are the part of ourselves
   that has retained our memory and focus.
Keeping us aligned with the mission of our coming
   into this reality of separation.
For us they were both
   the Image and the Prototype of our man-forms.

Diligently they set about to create a reality
More separate from the Source than We had ever been before.

To return home like a boomerang was their goal.

They saw
That as We moved to the furthest point

Where the separation would be so great,
We would create so much momentum,
By our own dynamic tension,
    that there would be a rush to return
        from our self-made oblivion.

They believed that All That Is Us would create
    a wonderful drama that would, in the end,
        return us all home again.

So this is what they-We have done-become.

And they started immediately.

First they looked throughout Lyra's newly formed star system,
Seeking planets ripe for the manipulation of energy.
Looking to densify matter to create physical beings,
Flesh-and-blood vehicles that would become the means
    to carry our We-ness the furthest from the Source.

The Founders were our older Brothers and Sisters.
They were like our parents, too.
Like Sky Father and Earth Mother who held onto the blueprint,
They followed their inclination, their guidance,
    to nurture the newness and hold on to the focus.

And in so doing they became the blueprint
    encoding within their spirit form
        the future of all of the fragments We would become.

The Founders understood the patterns of the energy developing.
They stood in the integrated place between positive and negative.
Creator's paradigm was presented and they comprehended
    (while most did not)
        that our fragmented pieces of consciousness
            must merge and return to our birth.

They said:

> "When a civilization chooses integration (and it is only a
> matter of time when it will), it will naturally move toward the
> neutral point. Never further apart. For a civilization to make
> such a leap, the people will have to make the connection that
> further apartness-making will only accommodate the denial of

> *their opposite, causing more pain and dysfunction for them-*
> *selves. Creating a condition that is abnormal and disharmonious*
> *with our Creator's Plan."*

The painful experience would end, they saw.
One way or the other it would end.

And so,
The Founders were poised with their understanding,
Watching as the rest of the Whole
    became curious about the future.

At that instant they caused themselves to fragment again.
Dispersing themselves and their locked focus
Into holographic shards that scattered
    throughout all of the newly unfolding Is-ness.
Embedding themselves into every aspect of creation.

Birthing infinite numbers and varieties of themselves,
    into every reality to come.

Just like the Fallen Ones they were. Only different.
The Founders' sacrifice knew the plan and knew who they were.
More importantly, they knew where We were going.

And because of this fragmentation. This consciousness action.
They assured all of creation on this side of the veil
That every part of ourselves would be a part of themselves,
And that all of creation would know the plan.

That God would be seen in the eye of a fly.

The Founders had diminished themselves
    in whole-completeness numbers.

Even so, there remained behind
    many of their members who became
        part of the fifty-two to be named
            the great ancient families of legend and myth.
Standing by to assist all of creation from time to time.
Helping All That Is Us back to the line
    that leads to our home in our Creator's heart.
        The hearth of our beginnings.

****

Part IV

Sister Lyra and Brother Vega

Lyra

In the beginning it was Lyra and Vega
    that began the clock of hu-man illusion.
These stars gave all of themselves
    to our earliest lineage-heritage.
This place in the sky was the womb-cradle home
    of the humanoid race.

The newly formed stars watched as We slowly became aware
    of our place in this Time-Space.
Our self-inflicted shock had diminished.
    Our stunned continence sought fulfillment-movement.
      Our first attempts at reconciliation had begun.

But without form, heart, fingers or toes,
    all We had was our imagination
      which sensed the end, but could not see the path.

We bumbled and stumbled
    creating dissension among ourselves.
Our largeness diminished as groups separated themselves
Into smaller, more manageable cliques of righteousness.
And our elder Brothers and Sisters, the stars,
    assured us that now was the moment
      to descend deeper into density.
We needed to freeze-frame our co-creation for a time,
    in order to grow out of our diversity.

The stars stood patiently by, watching our dis-focused efforts
Working in the etheric-physical planes.
Watching as We played with forms and ideals.

Of course, We did not think our efforts so small.
Nor did they, but they did see
That our impetuous programs
Would take longer to complete
Than one concerted motto ought to.

The Logos spoke and the stars sang,

> *"All shall return to the Source.*
> *All shall evolve.*
> *In every way ye shall experience and grow.*
> *Physically, Mentally, Spiritually, and Emotionally.*
> *Of this We shall assure."*

The seeding had begun.

With permission from the Source
The Founders had dispersed themselves
    throughout all of Creation.
Embedding a portion of their own being
    into all things that had gone on before.
Their Psalm of Integration was sung.
Their need to co-create balance to our creation was fulfilled.

Grand was their plan, assuring our completion.

It was a portion of the Founders' group consciousness,
Containing all seven octaves of expression,
That had blasted and fractured the Void.
Their elements flew about the galaxies and universes
Attracting themselves to like-vibrational, heavenly bodies,
Embedding themselves into every new-born planet and sun.

Their hologram shards had found physical and etheric abodes
    of matching frequency everywhere.
No part of Creation was left untouched.
The broth now seasoned was ready for us.

Barren planets began to display
First and second density forms of life.
The Founding part of ourselves had used the primal codes
To quasi-reproduce themselves.
Replications that would occur nonetheless,
Now assured of their blueprinted awareness.
They had carefully placed portions of themselves
Far below their natural state.
Further embedding the plan.

Rememberest thou the maxim,
    Life begets life in a give-away manner?
      Here is where it began.

'Round about Lyra the Founders made ready
Multitudinous planets for their consciousness to join.
They seeded these planets and nurtured them quickly,
Working diligently they fed
    the naturally developing primate life-forms
        with pieces and chunks of themselves.
Infusing directly their own GEM-coded DNA
    into the etheric and physical bodies of the young apes.
A model they would repeat over and over again.
One that We would later use, when We would play God.

Indigenous life flourished on the planets
With man-like species developing quickly,
Becoming,
    forefathered templates of the humanoid race.

All at once life appeared
Throughout all of the worlds of the universe.
Time wasn't a reality just yet.
Karma was just being birthed.

The Founders then selected those species
That could make tools and dig roots,
And withstand the pain of the growth of a large brain.
Our Godparents nurtured and fed them
And encouraged them to grow and become,
    until they made fire.
Thus signaling to everyone that these creatures were aware.
That they were ready for the moment of the I AM.
The wisdom of the Shakti day.

It took many thousands of years
For the apes' second-density brains
To merge with the higher awareness
Of third- and fourth-density consciousness.
We could see them now.
We understood what the Founders had done.

We saw this creature was exactly
The means to carry us back home.
And We lowered our vibrations
From seventh to sixth to fifth to fourth.

Passing through the veils of three heavens
into the first hell.

We hovered there as the young Two-Leggeds
Gained wisdom and culture and grew in size and stature.
We worked with the body and the mind
Of this creature called Man.
Feeding our own etheric genetics into them.
Making them more like ourselves.

We learned to love our co-creation.
And We flirted with consciousness infusion,
As We embedded aspects of ourselves
Into the chakras and glands of the animal body.

And then we waited.

****

In the beginning the creature was slow and clumsy.
It wasn't able to grasp grand concepts.
It was stubborn and dull.
It was not a compliant host for our quickening at all.

It wasn't long, however,
Maybe a hundred Sidereal cycles or so,
Before Lyran-Man was flirting with space travel.
Growing in intellect and genetic-memory awareness,
Unlearning, but never forgetting his baser instincts.
Never forgetting from whence he had come.

And Lyran-Man did not forget The Plan.
The Founders had seen to that.
Totally aware of their beginnings
And able to see the probable end,
The Lyrans created much anguish for themselves.

Some planet groups were content
With the life they gifted themselves,
Seeing little more that they could do
But to wait for the their species to evolve.

Some of our fellow experimenters
Found the experience too painful;
Their vibrational patterns

Were disharmonious with the physical.
They abandoned the Lyran-Man,
  Returning to the etheric,
    To be more in control of their destiny.
Penetrating other planets
  That were more suited to themselves.
    Traveling on their own thought-waves.

Soon the entire Lyran star system was saturated
With a thousand diverse groups of man-species.
Mocking what some have said:
    that man was created in the image of God.
When in fact it is more accurate to say
    that the image of God was given to man.
All is an illusion, you see.

The first manifestation of electromagnetic expression appeared.
The poles of the magnet were found.
The electron of action-reaction was sparked.
Passive magnetics and aggressive electricity were birthed.
Fire and water were separated.

It is important to know that each of the planets in this,
Our first star system,
Were homogeneous in and of themselves.
They were comprised of like-minded thinking.
The planet itself saw to that.
Expelling or ending vibrational disharmony
That partook of its sustenance.

In time, however,
As the Lyran-Man evolved, his ideas molted.
Polarization began to create schisms in his civilizations.
Colonies were formed of more specialized like-minded citizens.

Disharmony began to flourish amongst the people.
The nurturing female drifted further into compliance.
And the dominant male was all too eager to fill the void.

As they began to experience their various ideas,
Their diversity increased in physicality.
Multiple races and species variations were encouraged,
Thinking that this was the way to get back home.

It wasn't sudden, without warning,
    this plan of forced dysfunction.
There was no escaping it.
We were ALL Gods, you see.
We were the Angels of Creation
    and this was the moment We had waited for.
All of us thought it would be settled soon.
But the Founders knew that it would be
    the first of an eternity of trials.

And so, the entire Lyran culture of exactness
    became embroiled in violent wars of "Correctness."

And the more diverse We became.

Planets became homes to our differences.
The man-form was firmly established
    and flourished by our consciousness.
We could now say,
    "They were We and We were them."

And more developed We became.

The body adapted to our focus.
The mind coordinated our fingers
As We built magnificent machines,
    to transport our bones,
        our genetics finely honed
            to neighboring planets and stars.

And in the process,
We had quickly exhausted the organics of our worlds.
We had burned to extinction the decayed thought-forms,
The tree and the fern, that became our coal and oil.

And then We reached out to conquer the skies.

The secret of the Atom We knew,
For the Atom was us in a singular form.
The energy leaked in abundance
And We contained its heat behind shields of pure density.
We boiled the plasmatic essence in liquid flux
And by its exhaust We traveled,
Impulse-propelled through the heavens,

Leaving sickness and death in our wake.
Our home-worlds were rid of us.
Uninhabitable to all life below the fourth.

And We warred amongst ourselves
and the others that We found in our way.
    "Our way is best," We cried.
        "Our way will lead us back."
We did not know that We were no longer One.

Stupid, We saw most of the others to be.
Ignorant and savage they were.

"All is a tool for Us to use!" We yelled.
"Greater than you We are." We thought.
"Of higher mind and purpose are We." We lied.
"Submit to our greatness. Comply with our ways! Or else!"

It didn't work.

Deeper and deeper We fell into differences.
Each planet's races were too diverse.
They looked different from us.
We had to protect our genetics.
We had to remind ourselves over and over again:
    "Our form is most pleasing to our Source.
        "Everyone knows that!"

Bigotry of race had begun.
Even though culture and language were the same.
We had forgotten that We were the same. Almost.

It was the planets' environments
    that created the different textures of hair and skin.
It was the sun's light that affected the coloring of the eyes.
It was the body that was only doing what was right for itself,
Else it would die and the experiment would end.

Thank the Founders that spirit-made-manifest
Continued to hold onto its form.

Because We were dealing with the reality of polarity.
Over a period of time various separations occurred
As the Children of Creation began to diverge.

And the challenge to work with this dissimilarity
    pushed at our attempt for unity.

It was not as easy as it sounds, to heal the breach,
And there were many wars within Lyra's star's reach.
Wars were created for the control
    of the method to come home.
We fought for the domination of our god-given right
    to expand our self-righteous ideas.
To make the others see the folly of their ignorance.
And We were determined to make it so.

No less like the TV preacher-man
Who would speak Love from one side
Of his prophet-quoting mouth
And Hell's damnation from the other,
Did We seem to be shouting mixed messages.
As well as killing one another in the name of All-That-Is.

Creation was now out of control.
The Founders could no longer monitor the change.
The child had run away from its hearth.
They who had nurtured the new birth
Could only watch in astonishment
As We wrote and re-wrote our history.
The ending was assured,
    the moral was the theme.
        The versions never ceased.

In deep despair We might have doubted
That the end could ever be reached.
But the solar flare of every planet's sun reminds us
That as it leaps far from its Source,
It is immediately caught in gravity's attraction
    and sucked back into the seething cauldron's fire.
It matters not how far the flame vomits from the mass,
It returns.
By the mass gravity of the greater whole
It returns.
Our Source will never abandon us.
By our venturous pilgrimages it lives.

We are the Prodigal Son.

****

Vega

Within the Lyran system there were many star groups.
One such cluster came to be called Vega.

Vega was different from the other stars.
It pushed at our senses to display aggression,
>the masculine polarity.
That was its nature.
>Its rise in influence was long overdue.

Elsewhere it was the Lyrans that spawned
The more nurturing and feminine nature of ourselves.
Their fault was that the sameness persisted,
>even though the cultures grew and mixed
>>and even warred amongst themselves.
It was more a conflict of semantics than territory.
Yet, even that was untrue.

We continued to search among ourselves
For the correct amalgamation
That would transcend our status and hasten our return.
It was inevitable that internal differences
>would become more noticeable,
That bigotry and other aberrant behavior would grow.
Nonconformity was discouraged, even repressed.
The noncompliant aggressive left our presence in Lyra
And migrated to the favorable pulse-resonance of Vega.
Where *Self* could flourish with vigor.

Certain groups of consciousness were forced to become aware
>that their philosophies were different.
And the first division between ourselves had appeared.
They took their ships of space and fled to Vega.
Others traveled to other star systems
>and became lost for a time.

It wasn't long before the wars
Between the Lyrans and Vegans had begun.
The war between our forefathers and mothers

Increased in its earnest intensity.
These warring siblings would be the very same Gods
That would torment and tease us throughout all Time.
They were only us,
    twenty-two civilizations removed.

****

It has been said, "As above, So below."
The patterns We experience here on our Earth
Were encoded within us by our parents.
Their etheric DNA is ours.
There is no separation from the Source at this level.
It is a memory of dysfunction that deliberately devolved itself.
And they couldn't reconcile
Their differences with their neighbors in a good way.
Is there any difference today?

The wars between the Gods were more frightening to behold
Than any fought by man.
But no worse than pulling the wings off a fly.
Starting from most high, traveling to the most low,
The memories were carried in hopes
That All That Is would evolve and recombine.
Becoming more aware than It ever was before.
And We The Angels have been carrying and nurturing,
Rebirthing and repeating all of our fathers' follies
All of this time.

> "*Dearly beloved,*" Spake the great historian Germane,
> "*if you wish to shed your coded entrapments, you can if you
> understand their nature and source. Understand them well
> enough, and recognize their root urgings and promptings.
> When you do this you will cease falling victim to them.*"

This is the way the great masters were taught
    to take control of the patterns and codings
        that hold fast to their emotional bodies.
The only part of us that is carried from life to life.
The only source of joy and sorrow
    that can cloud our judgment
        and temper our experience.

These codes are not blueprinted to be lived anew.
They are not an astrological path of fate or point-of-view,
Or the numerological patterning of propensity,
Locked in the GEMS of our being from the moment of birth.
They are simply there.
And they are triggered when our emotions
Remember similar situations that sparked reactions,
Which may or may not have been
Healthy for the mind or the body at that time.

An understanding of etheric bleed-throughs
Will be needed in the days to come.
The multidimensional self that we are
Exists everywhere all at once.
Time is not a factor here. Time is karma's history.
The clock is always standing still
When the old patterns are discovered and shed
      from the newly created spirit-made-manifest
         that walks in third-density ignorance.

You see,
When We, the ignorant, decide not to do something
Because the urgings and promptings seem foreign to us,
We have stopped a primal action-reaction
      that is as old as creation itself.
Search for the source of your discomfort.
Find it and release it,
      and the totality all of your being will be healed.
History literally has been changed.
And all of us advance another step toward home.
Because an old, ancient pattern,
Birthed and embedded in Lyra and Vega,
      has been found and released.

We can transmute our species through fresh, conscious actions.
Cleansing ourselves of our ancient patterning.
Shattering old beliefs and beau ideals.
Bringing Sumafi and Vold-ness to all of creation.
This is what they, our forefathers,
Have been attempting to do from the beginning of time.
This is what We will do for them.

If you understand the totality of this premise,
All of totality will be changed.

****

And so it was that our fathers and mothers,
The Vegans and Lyrans,
Manifested the humanoid races which would become
Prototypes for all of the others that followed.

The etheric-physical beings of Lyra
That expressed service to others
Made homes for their consciousness in the fair-skinned,
Light-eyed, humanoids that lived on the cloudier worlds.

The physical-etheric beings of Vega
That expressed service to self
Made homes for their consciousness in the darker-skinned,
Dark-eyed humanoids that lived on less watery worlds.

This was how race consciousness had begun,
Where We and They could be identified
        by color of skin and texture of hair.
As the role playing of passive and aggressive
        corrupted all who played the game.
An arrogance of existence and superiority
        sparked between them.

An idea of handsome and ugly had blossomed.

The Lyrans in the beginning were not very aggressive,
        possessing a feminine or intuitive nature.
The group in the Vegan area were more masculine.
More aggressive and warlike, needing to expand and conquer.

This, then, became the boil-root source of the conflict
        between the Lyran-Vegan peoples.
Both had conquered space and technology.
Both were tight-fistedly holding
Onto their own distortion of the Law of One.
Then, after aeons of time,
Their spiritual and philosophical differences
Became more pronounced

And the wars became mindless Jihads
   of death and destruction.

The Founders saw the experiment take on a mind of its own.
They knew that eventually it would be a success.
They knew mankind must grow apart
Before it could grow back together.

It wasn't pleasant this apartness-making.
There were many wars, with many planets destroyed.
And throughout every single conflict and emotional outburst,
The genetic tendency of the two forms of aggression
Was embedded further into our being.
Left to us Earthlings to resolve
For the sake of our celebrated, celestial ancestors.

And the Founders watched in sadness
As the Eden-like worlds of our fathers were destroyed.

They saw that this road would lead to no end.
They flexed their collective wings and searched the area,
And found a planet just right nearby.
One that could house all of the diverse races and ideas
That were raging on the home worlds of Lyra and Vega.
And they called the planet the Apex.
The trinary Apex of unity where positive and negative
Would be given a fresh chance to become whole again.

It was a thought that would be repeated time and again.
But this was the focus that the Founders maintained
And they would not be denied.

****

And so the growing epic, like a live cancer,
Was transplanted to the Apex,
Where it would emerge thousands of lifetimes later
As an example unrepeatable of survival.

In the interim
There were those who chose not to content themselves
   with watching its evolution.
They left Lyra completely
   to make their own story of integration.

They saw -- or thought they saw --
　　a better outcome of their decision.
They did not understand then,
　　nor would they understand later,
The Law of Probable Realities.

Another gift from Chaos.

　　　　　　　　**********

Part V

The Apexian Epic

And the wars and rumors of wars spread throughout Lyra,
    as the Founders searched the nearby Galaxies
        for the planet just right, to begin afresh
        the mating of our differences.
A place where the conflict would be resolved
    and peace, for a time, could live.

And found they, in a place geometrically correct.
A grouping of stars and a planet they named the Apex.

To some it was just a glittering dust-speck
Caught in the milky ebb of galaxies newly created.
To the Founders
It was a world perfectly placed and fully formed,
Waiting anxiously for co–creators' inhabitants.
Waiting to manifest the final resolution
    to the growing problem.

Events then unraveled so fast, so quickly,
That the interim was seldom remembered.
The events had become blurred, but not forgotten,
Because the Apex was still close to the source, the beginning.

From an idea, to a form, it began.
So quickly it had occurred and without discussion,
That even today to remember causes mass confusion.

Still, there is no doubt that they, on that day,
Created, with our assistance,
Another beginning of our existence.

For the third time.

Again, We called this the beginning of ALL Time as We reckon.
The beginning when God was still making decisions.
Back in the days when We were God,
Making imperious, delicious determinations.

Expecting each one to live to its final conclusion.
To live correctly our idea of how it should be done.

****

The Founders felt that the Apex
Would quickly solve our differences.
At least they thought that it would be so.
At least they hoped that it would be so.
Because as they had watched the Lyrans and Vegans,
Leave their home worlds devastated and blasted,
Going elsewhere to lick their wounds,
They felt sorrow's compassion swell in their breasts.
They found that they were now linked
   to the deep-density seeding
      they had spread throughout all of Creation.
And they knew that Creation was becoming aware of itself,
Even as the first family of man began to scatter askew.

Lyra and Vega had been failures.
   "How can that be!?" We cried.
The answer We knew within ourselves.
The question was mootingly pouring from our toxic exhausts,
As We fled from our wasted homelands.
Taking our biases with us.

And so the Founders called out
To the remaining Vegans and Lyrans, saying:

> *"Brothers! Sisters!*
> *We have found the Apex.*
> *The polarity point of balance.*
> *It has the harmonics to mend your discord.*
> *Come and see for yourselves!"*

Then they waited and watched
As our Vegan Brothers and Lyran Sisters, ourselves,
   turned our attention to the Apex.

The Apex, tucked away in Lyra's star clusters,
Desperately wanted to please.
And soon it was seeded with our own spark essences.
Beginning Creation again.

The Founders watched as the races,
    represented in glorious profusion,
Explored and defused into their new homeland.

And for a time the Apexians lived well.
Perhaps a half sidereal cycle or so.

The conflict, however, brooded and simmered,
As the dispersion of the differences continued.
And they heard rumors of injustices that were inflicted
Upon their departed relatives.
The ones who went to Sirius, Altair and Centauri.
And many of them stewed in their imagined indignity.
    Paranoia's best friend.

Soon this, the third civilization of Creation,
Could not hold the rope of reintegration.
And it began to unravel like the ball of twine
Tumbled about by a cat.
It fell apart in warring factions, all together swearing:
    "Do it MY way.
        My way will lead us back!"

This saw, now old, its teeth blunted,
chipped away at the last of the civilization that would cry,
    "Peace, Brother and Sister! Let us make peace,
        so that We might enjoy our liberty."

To no avail.
The enforced copulation
    of a thousand philosophies escalated
        and in the end
Killed many, many milliards of the Creator's flesh children.

The sensitive souls retreated in shock.

It was fusion's reaction and a nuclear war
That forced the surviving population underground.

Some were barely able to escape in fright,
    as strength against strength blew their World apart.
Took they with them the survivors' guilt question.
Saying over and over again,
    "We are Gods, are We not?

We are correct, while they are not.
Why can't We live together in peace?"

Plaintive was their moan of self-righteous indignation.
Great was their fear that they had destroyed
    everything that was their good life.

Looking back We/They saw the future disarrayed,
And those who had stayed behind
Decided to live their price,
Aloof and untainted by wars and strife;
They decided to make an existence
That they could call the good life... Again.
Good-for-what would soon be determined,
    for during the interim
        everything but survival would be seconded.

And the third day of creation had passed
    into the long night of regret.
The Apex had fallen apart in destruction.

For, you see, accustomed as We were to getting our way,
We found that others wished dominance to do
    as We ourselves had thought right.
And We forgot Love and Light.
    We sought only Life and Law,
        the shortcut to the abyss,
            not the All.

The Apex disintegrated and many had fled
    in close-minded thought-form cliques
        to establish their own colonies of obedience.
And they found that the more they tried for conformity-unity,
The further they traveled from the Source.
And the lament of the failed was heard
Throughout all of the Cosmos:

        "O God, My Father-Mother,
why am I cursed with the direction that no one follows?
I pray that they let ME show them the light.
Why don't they understand what they do?
I see the folly of their creation.
Forgive me, Creator, for I now know what to do.

I must show them their digressions,
the errant course of their wayward directions.
Incredible as it seems,
I am the only one who sees
the misguided transgressions that they lead.

"It is the others who have failed, not me."

And the darkness enveloped all of Creation,
As the minds of Gods continued to play with separation.

****

The third attempt at Civilization was finished.
Or at least it seemed so at the time.
As Lyra and Vega smoldered on the horizon,
The planet Apex was stinking
    of decayed flesh and fractured rock.
The surface was destroyed, completely,
    wiped out by the free electrons unleashed
        from the nasty bombs and torpedoes built to kill
            everything that breathed and walked on the surface.
The radiation had penetrated miles into the crust.
Nearly reaching the many who had escaped
    down the mine shafts and volcanic fissures
        to live in the phosphorous-illuminated caves and caverns
        far below the surface.

They were the refugees who refused to leave the planet
    when the wars ripped apart
        the city-states that flourished throughout the land.
They felt they were destined to resolve the Apexian plan,
Showing the rest of us the *way* to live in peace.
Noble, they thought they were.

Out of lonely loyalty to the cause they supported,
The survivors had gone underground.
To hide until the half-life
Of the ugly, slow death had transpired.
And they could return to the surface again.

The planet, utterly destroyed, floated in space.
Too hot to come near.

Quarantined by the deadly, toxic rays themselves,
Their home had become a memory to the rest of the Cosmos.

Forgotten. Written off as a disaster not to be repeated.
The rest of us had left to find new worlds to conquer.
We never thought again about those We had left behind.
But they never forgot us.

Deep into the thick crust of the planet they had disappeared.
Where they lived off the hydroponic gardens that thrived
In the eerie light of boiled, incandescent, vapored minerals.
And they breathed the filtered air
Continually recycled by the atomic engine-generators
That ran silently for more than 1,000 millennia.

The Apexians,
Highly skilled engineers and technicians,
Inventors of machines and devices that would become
The archetypes of everything to be created by future man,
Were the first species to alter themselves in appearance
        simply by growing a larger intellect.

Long before their planet's surface was destroyed,
their features began to take on a top-heavy appearance.
Their craniums grew larger
To accommodate their expanding brains.
Brains that housed the knowledge
        of their long-lived lifetimes.

For they did live a long time.
And in this, their memories, their experiences
Were always first-lived, personal knowings.
Seldom had they needed to pass on their stories.
They were living their myth.

Great, great, great-grandfather and mother
Knew their grandchildren personally.
They were able to teach the children
        the mechanics of all things
That made their lifestyle possible and exciting.

But they had become too quickly bored.
They had indulged themselves in the mind-altering chemicals
        that placed them in dysfunctional states,

Where their minds caused them to rehearse and replay
    the beginnings of our Universe.
Where they belabored over and over again
    the correctness of their decision
        to be the solution to the Lyran-Vegan question,
Where We and they,
    you and I,
        could become one. Again.

They were gone from their bodies most of the time.
Expanding their minds, obsessing on knowledge;
Finding new ways to reconcile their differences.
Inventing new machines to pamper their existence.
They had become addicted to their superior intellect.
They were supra-mind.
And their self-pleasured arrogance
    became self-contamination
        as they began to change their appearance.

The more intelligent they became,
The more lost in their greater brains were they.
Not lost as We know it.
But stuck in a place
That might seem to us
The answer to OUR integration,
    but was in fact a labyrinth of no escape.
All of co-creation at that time
    was stuck in the same mindset.
The experience was different for each of us.
The "no-end" was the same.
    That is why We had left.
    And why they had stayed.

And so the Apex
And its underground peoples were abandoned.
A devastated monument to "no-future."
Leaving the survivors of invention,
The ones with the large craniums,
To face their own certain extinction,
    because they could no longer birth children.
The unborn babies' heads, you see,
    were too large for their mothers' pelvic passages.

Birth was only possible by surgery.
Which became a blasphemy to skewed purists,
    who said:

"In utero we grow.
It is not natural to cut out the fetus like a festering cancer.
Better we should learn the techniques of fertilization
And nurture a child in a glass of fluid
Than disgrace our women with the scars of surgery
Or worse,
Allowing the birth process to tear both apart,
Causing agony and death to mother and child,
Just to maintain a semblance of naturalness.

"Our minds have caused us to grow.
We must give up the old birth process.
It served our ancestors well. But it is killing us."

And the Apexians moved further from reality.
Choosing to keep their form of expression,
    their body-type of experience,
They altered their ancestral, procreation process.

And the grandmothers wept, as they saw
    there was no other choice for their daughters.

In elaborate ceremony, witnessed by all of the clan,
A handsome mother, dressed in the sheerest of gossamer,
Would ascend the seven steps of the rainbow platform,
To walk seven times around the alabaster and ebony altar,
Humming the mantra of lullaby's cradlesong.

When the prayer was done
She would lie on the raised dais' cold stone
Solemn silence filling the hall.
The priest-scientists would surround her
And quickly extract the developing fetus
Placing it in a vat of amber fluid
    to be fed until the full term was met.

But even this festival of birth became too much to bear.
The grandmothers and grandfathers said:

"Too much!
We are in pain to see our unborn children

Living the last of their prebirth existence
Within the walls of a glass uterus.
Change the process!
If we die, we will. If we live, we will.
But this ... is .... too much!
Our excesses have been our death!

"We've seen it!
We are a people who must live to tell our story!
    Can you not find another way to keep us alive?
    Another way to allow us to survive?"

It was the saddest day of their sad history
When the scientists, the priests and the mothers convened
The last of the Fetualical Grand Councils.
The Councils whose duty it was to choose
    the future mothers of their race.

This was their decision:

They would continue to perform the ritual
    of procreation-extraction for appearances' sake.
While behind the curtains of the temple structures
    they would birth replicas of themselves.
Imbued with the genetics of their kind,
New vessels made ready for the waiting spirits.
Made from blood and tissue
    and not by the issue of the womb.
They were to become the masters of the first kind.
Creating third-density life from nothing.

This, then, was the process they brought underground
    along with their machines and their memories.
And here they lived.
    Not happily, but forever.

Their wish had been granted.
Immortality was guaranteed and they settled into their fate,
Knowing that as soon as their planet's surface cooled
They might return to the above and begin their lives again.

But Chaos would have none of that.
Chaos said:

"You have destroyed your home.
You have altered yourselves.
You are no longer Apexians!
You are the sons and daughters of mind-driven excess.
You have become someone else!

"So be it!

"Live, then, and reap the fruits of your minds.
Not cursed as you understand it.
Just different, to experience the plan."

Baffling was the message of Chaos,
The dis-structure that ruled without malice.
The Creator of All That Is.

****

Imperious decisions were made deep within the caverns,
And as replicated life stewed in the holy vats,
Other parts of the Apexian existence became threatened.
First they found that the neutrinos of their beings
Had been altered by the prolonged exposure on the surface.

They were sterile. Their heads were too big,
Their pelvic passages too small.
They were dwarfed, sterile freaks
With no reason for existence at all.

Yet exist they did,
Confident that they would overcome their
radiated self-made oblivion.
And the ritual of life-making became
The celibate chore of the scientist-priests.
The caring for the newborn, the task of the priestesses.
The training of the children, the chore of the community.

Love was no longer necessary.
And without Love, there was no passion.
And without passion there was no Light.
Illumination had ceased.
All that was left was Law and Life.
Spirituality, the celebration of being,
      had become the religion of avoiding death.

So focused were they on keeping secure
Their need to solve the challenge of integration,
They became the masters of dysfunction.
Each was one part of the whole.
The whole was nothing but sameness.
Our Brother and Sister angels of creation,
    had slipped into the oblivion
        of mind-created, lock-step conformity,
Where their creetch-born offspring
    knew nothing of hugs or embraces,
        kisses or tears,
            the needs or wants of their own.
Just survival of the clan.

The Apexians became like the ants of humankind.
Worse! They lacked even a queen!
All were the same.
They had become a WE of the first distortion.
There was no "you and I," to reconcile.
They were fated never to know birth again.
They were fated never to know passion.
Of this they had made certain.

You see,
As the time passed beneath the surface,
The scientists and priests schemed
To permanently remove the source of their emotions.
They found a way to shunt the lower chakric centers,
Blocking a portion of the original light frequency
    that imbued the consciousness with the zest for life.

This was not as difficult as it seems.
Their reproductive organs had atrophied from lack of use.
The gonadal hormones no longer spiced their blood.
Other vital organs fell into disuse
    as their diet became less and less dependent
        on the food of their gardens,
And more dependent on absorbing the energy given
    by the luminiferous rocks of their caves.

They were being metamorphosed
By the phosphorous-rich lichen that covered the walls.

Their features were changing.
The lack of sunlight altered their skin and their eyes.
Their scientists worked quickly to adapt the newly born
To the genetics of the evolving ones.
Changing more quickly than evolution would have done,
    they created a new species, life-form.

Missing their lower chakras and having altered brains
    that would never be affected again
        by the adrenal rushes of emotion and passion,
The genetic engineers shut off the "I AM" juices from their egos.
They removed certain portions of their DNA strands,
    making them different from the Founders' blueprinted plan.

The clones, like guinea pigs,
Evolved by the dispassionate efforts of scientist-priests.
Until the very core of their beingness, awareness,
    was now under control.

They had become a sentient "group mind."
Of intellect so superior they never missed
    their individual expressions.

Or so they thought.

****

There once was a people a long time ago, who,
    in their arrogance, pushed at their reality
and became lost in the manipulation of their existence.
    Becoming victims of their single-minded madness.
        The Founders, acting for Creator
    made for them a planet, a place called The Apex.
            Said They:

*"Here you will work through your apartness.
        Here you have the license
            to create or destroy,
                grow or wilt,
    become more or become less of yourselves."*

****

The Apexian ancestry is ours to learn.
In their story lives a lesson of immense dimension.
It was within the Lyran system that a planet developed
Becoming very diverse from all of its neighbors.

It was peopled by pacifists and warriors
Of all colors and shapes.
It was hoped, by the Founders,
To be the final solution,
    the planet of our integration;
Where differences and diversity could be reconciled
    and unified into a whole thought again.

It was the Apex, very similar to Earth.
It became the melting pot for the genetics of the Universe.
    Just like the Earth.

But the similarities did not end there.
Their surface society had manifested
A great deal of individuality called diversity.
Far more intense than what Earth has now.
Every polarity was expressed on the Apex.
Every idea was allowed to flourish,
But none was allowed to control.
Thus the disharmony began to grow.
Because the beings could not change as quickly as the ideas.
Old patterns, even then, were hard to shake.
And then the gap between the cultures widened.

Pollution.
The direct offspring of disharmonious thought,
Clouded their skies.
Severe toxicity rained down upon their planet,
Poisoning their rivers and lakes.
The animals and plants of their world began to disappear.
And then the serious wars began.
As radiation from high-yield atomics
    ravaged their own kind.

Pollution.
The atmosphere was dying.
The plant life was not producing oxygen.
We have seen the same caused by our fossil-fueled engines.

It would be hard for us to imagine pollution of a kind
That was birthed in our thoughts.
But that is what dis-eased consciousness does.
Affecting the living first- and second-density life forms.
The lower forms of Life that We,
    in our ignorance-arrogance, can judge.

And the Apexians watched the air that they breathed
    and the fluids that they drank
        become a sepiated broth of murky stench,
Contaminated by their perceptions of greater-than-you-ness.
Twiddling their collective thumbs,
While the fungus, the creepy crawlies,
The homeless unshaven and bag-ladies died mysteriously,
They watched their planet mirror their own imbalance.

Sound familiar?

Thus they evolved.

First they looked to technology to save them.
Until their own natural evolution caused deaths at birth.
Their population decreased.
Next they found themselves experiencing
The planetary-wide catastrophe of war and famine
And they foresaw the eventual destruction of their species.
Desperation forced them to clone their offspring,
Eliminating forever the natural birth process.

Some fled to other star systems to be lost in the mists of time.
The remainder went underground to escape the toxins,
And they took their engineered children with them.
The stars were lost from their eyes.
All there was, was the rock.
    Their Mother, the Earth.

Caverns were hewn from the mantle.
Like termites in concrete they cocooned themselves
Snugly within their underground cities,
Where they developed alternative energy sources
That did not rely upon sunlight, carbon or oxygen.
Thus they created a place that was autonomous,
    free of the surface eco-system.

They taught us
That a body can adapt to an environment without sun
And by genetic manipulation they could change
The DNA codes the children would become.
Making them indigenous to any sunless,
    treeless, underground world.

Their skin absorbed frequencies of light
That were not seen, but felt.
And from that absorption came heat and life.
They ate the nutrients from the luminiferous rocks,
And from the plants that glowed in the dark.
They bred the fish that swims in blackness.
They allowed themselves to become these qualities.

Large-eyed, pale of skin. Small in stature.
They eventually became adjusted to their new home.
The thick mantle of the planet itself,
    protected them from their toxic past.

This was their existence.
For thousands of years they had lived in their self-made exile.
Until one day, when the scientists determined
That the half-life of the atomics' radiation
Had dissipated to a level of tolerance they could withstand,
They sent their scouts to the surface.
The "Group We" had made a decision!
They would return to the above
    and rebuild their cities of splendor!

And they found something more painful
than anything they had previously experienced.

They were no longer Apexians!

Their star and galaxy had rejected them!
They were released from their homeland.
Cast-off from their fabled place in the heavens.
They were a ship of lepers.
    And they were alone.

The absolute worst fate that could have happened
To the "Group We".

Their creetch-mind screamed in agony.
Cut off from their heritage, their connection to the Source.

When they ventured to the surface they found
    that the breakdown of molecular matter
       had penetrated the subatomic levels
Creating an electromagnetic warp in their time-space fabric.
Their planet had shifted into an alternate, dimensional reality!

Their sun had ripped their planet from its orbit
And cast them into oblivion.
Into another realm that could deal
With their toxicity and pollution.
The planet no longer existed in Lyra!

It had been moved to a binary star system.
The one We call Zeta Reticuli.

So foreign were the stars that greeted them,
that many released their souls from their bodies.

    "Cursed," they said they were. "Our bodies are cursed!
    Our minds are trapped in a flesh and blood vessel.
    We are nothing but a spore of the universe.
    Our place in the fabric of the cosmos
    Is warped beyond recognition.
    How can we possibly show others the way!
    When we, ourselves, have lost the Way!"

Those who came to the surface were so shocked
They left their bodies completely.
They went screaming to find an answer from the wise ones.
The Founders.

    "We kept the faith," they pleaded.
    "How could you have abandoned our cause?
    Could you not see that we
    Did everything we could to keep our home world intact?
    Are you a monster that enjoys our pain?
    Do you banish us to this wasteland of two stars
    That bleaches the last vestige of our existence
    Into a chlorinated, de-loused, tide pool of nothingness?
    Just to appease your plan!"

    "Are we nothing to you?"

The Founders who guarded the Gates of Time
Embraced the shattered souls that had endured their deaths.
They pulled within them the anguished ones
And showed them the consequences of Time's action.

The Founders spoke, saying:

> "Dearly beloved.
> You have been so puffed up in your arrogance.
> You missed the show of Time.
> Time has passed you by.
> So focused have you been on your plight,
> that you missed the pageant
> that paraded around you
> There is so much you need to learn.

> "Yes, even you,
> the technical geniuses of Creation,
> have never considered Time
> as a creature of cleansing and change.

> "Time and Space are very much like
> the curd of mother's milk.
> A cheese with holes and passages
> throughout its form.
> All planets and stars throughout all of Creation
> are connected to each other by
> the nonlineal tunnels and passageways
> of Space and of Time.

> "Your wounded planet has traversed
> a million years in Time to find
> a Space in which it can exist.
> She was only doing what was correct for her.
> Protecting the last of her children, yourselves;
> and the spirit essence of her body.

> "Don't be frightened.
> We have not forgotten you.
> You have found in your flight to reach us
> that Space will allow other means to reach your goal.
> Neither Time nor Space is a straight line,

and a line will never be
the fastest means to your destination.
It is the meandering path that fulfills the quest.
Which is the metaphor for life itself.

"You are the Phoenix.
You are the Apexians.
Out of your blanched world you will rise again,
to teach all of those who will stumble similarly
in the folly of certain directions
that can only lead to oblivion.

"You are the Ones who chose to show
the Universe the way to create
the ultimate reality of unity.
And by your example
others will be enlightened."

The Apexians were without speech.
They held fast to the Guardians of Time
And felt the connection to their beginnings
Pulsing warmly within their bosoms.
   "What can WE do?" they asked sadly.

Their question reeked of aeons of dwelling in self-pity.

A voice was heard from beyond the Gates of Time.
It was the Source, The Creator:

"First, My Children, you need to restore
that which your scientists removed from your bodies.
Too many were the directions your minds took.
Too many the inventions to ease your passage.
Those things are now your heritage,
to use to recapture your youth.
You have evolved differently from all of the rest.
That is Good!

"You have a message to impart.
That is Good!

"Remember your beginnings and your promise.
The reason for your sacrifice.
The reason your place
is no longer found in its niche in Time.

"Return to your people.
Take the knowledge that has been given.
Travel Time and Space.
Hold your place, steadfastly.
Find the Cup of Genetics that will restore your youth.
Evolve through your excess as the rest of Creation must do.
This goal,
held fast by my Guardians, is not reserved to the few!
ALL THAT IS must return to Me.
Any other idea is blasphemy."

The spirits of the departed Apexians returned to their people.
They brought the message from the Gates of Time.
They were to become the little ones
Of our dreams and nightmares.

They are the Zetas, the little people.
Thirty-three centimeters of ageless stature and wisdom,
Complete with large eyes and craniums,
And graceful thin arms and fingers.
They are what is left of a multitude of races.
Amalgamated into one kind of sameness.

****

News had spread among the survivors.
All at once, as was the nature of the "Group-Minded We."

They had changed themselves physically,
Altering both their emotional and mental bodies.
They decided that it was their emotions and their passions
That had driven them to destroy their planet's surface.
And they vowed that they would no longer allow
Either to abide in their minds.

They had violated a basic law of co-creation.
Depriving themselves of the passions of life.
Their experience was as bland, meek or humble
As a plastered wall or glass of water.
Having only one purpose to their being. To sustain life.
To live day-to-day without myth or reason,
Processing manufactured oxygen
And never knowing joy.

They knew they had succeeded when they had found
They no longer blinked or were overtly curious
When a stimulus came into their awareness.
They were completely emotionless.
A new race had been birthed.
They were more dead than alive.

Now, thousands of years later,
Caught in another Time-Space.
They had a decision to make.
Either they would recapture their youth
    and re-evolve to their present state,
Or forever be trapped in their flesh-made prison
Until the reason for their engineered duplication
    became lost in the sentient apathy of their group mind.

They could now, at this time, leave their bodies entirely
And join the etheric host of the Founders
And watch the progress of The Plan being lived
    by We, the Angels,
In the dimensions and densities below.
It was their stiff-necked intellect that pushed them to say, "No."

They were millions of years into their future
    and were without a past worth repeating.
Zeta Reticuli One and Two had burned their eyes,
    seared their skin,
        boiled the rocks and blasted the sand.
They were not indigenous to this star system.
It pulsed discomfortingly in their sensitive ears
That had long since learned
To hear inside the quiet of the caves.
Their minds were attuned to thoughts and soft breath.
Noise had not been allowed!
Their silence had been broken only by a click or a clack,
Never anything more than that!

And the winds on the surface had howled.
The movement of tectonic plates had thrust up new soil,
    grating their nerves.
It was pain they had felt again. And it was awful.
They felt driven to be somewhere else!
Their planet, their home was driving them away!

"What do we do?" they called out to the Guardians.
   "We do not know what to do!"

                    "Find your youth," came the answer.
                    "Remember your past and find your youth."

And so, from that day onward
They began to explore the Universe.
They had re-established their relations with the Founders,
And with the Guardians' blessings
They channeled all of their energies into genetic research.
To recreate themselves, naturally.
They had rediscovered their passion!

First, they wanted to learn
What they had done to themselves.
They realized they had made many mistakes.
They had become sterile from their own radiation.
They had become unable to reproduce naturally.
They had tinkered with their glandular systems
      breeding out their emotions.
They had eaten rocks, breathed processed air
      and bathed in the glow of phosphorous.
They were organic robots with the intellect of God.
They were freaks, weak and anemic,
      and completely unadaptable to their new environment.

And because of their knowledge of All That Is,
They were transitioning into the nonphysical
Etheric realms of fifth-density!
A place that would be welcomed by all of those
      who were evolving more naturally
            in the kingdoms and realms below.
But they knew how they had reached this place,
And it wasn't a group epiphany that had uplifted them;
It was their engineers and technicians
Who had altered their bodies.
It was their group mind that had bypassed their youth.
Too painful were the emotions of their ancestors,
And they obsessed on peace.
      Just as an addict would for drugs.

They had stopped themselves
From moving out of the fourth place
Because they realized they could not enter the fifth
Without first healing or transmuting
What they thought was their mistake.
From that time forward they have kept themselves
    from transitioning into nonphysicality.

They searched this new Universe for a gene pool
That would allow them to reintroduce
The DNA beads that they had removed from themselves.
Earth is one of the planets they have visited.
Earth contains all of the primary genetics
From their previous family of existence
Locked within one place.

They are the masters of Time and Space travel.
They can jump forward and backward at their will.
They search for the elusive answer to their predicament
And subtlely influence those whom they meet
To cease the development that would lead
To the dead end that they have become.

Their role is now well defined.
They look to their Oversoul,
The Founders (for they are One), for guidance
As they travel the Universes seeking the right combinations
Of the primal DNA strands
    to reintegrate their physical bodies.
By their own example of avoidance,
They find people everywhere to assist
In order to understand their own baser emotions.

They need to re-understand fear.
Just as We need to re-integrate ours.
Together, We and the little people will learn
    not to be victims and powerless again.

Their message is clear.

The spirit of the Apexian lives on all of the planets
    that are growing through similar conflicts and pollution.
Without their example, We would never know
    what fifteen million years in a cave will grow.

****

In the beginning, We agreed to experience All That Is.
And by so experiencing, We create even more ... All That Is.
And so it goes as it grows.

We all agreed to try every means of integration.
Some ways were painful, some were blithe.
Some ways were mean-spirited and took other's life.
Some were nurturing, denying self-liberty.
And some eliminated species reproduction,
Deciding that this would be the way to lead Us back home.

The Apexians had stopped birth to save their women's lives,
Celibates stop birth to save their essence for a higher cause.
What nobler cause is there, than to live and give birth?
To nurture the young?
Setting their feet firmly on the ground, saying:

> "Make of your life an example for the good of all.
> Live your life. Serve others as you serve yourself.
> Repeat no virtue or vice twice.
> Grow and become something greater
> than what you surrendered yourself to be."

The Apexians, friends from another time--
Ourselves, actually, when we were young--
Bypassed the lesson of emotion and passion.
They took the short-cut to bliss that was the abyss.
They are destined to be with us as long as We are with them.
Assuring that We will all return Home, together, again.

Unresolved is their example.
A loose end that is theirs to find and reweave
into their storybook tapestry of life.

Forgive them for their transgressions.
Their surgical implants,
Their late-at-night visits.
Their seemingly passionless probes and cuts.
Painful as they have been to you,
Consider the why beyond fear.
Help them to continue to piece together their youth.

Help their women know
The feel of movement in their wombs
And their men to pace the worried fathers' dance.
Help them to experience again
The first bloom of life, the cry of an infant,
Uniquely different from all of its kin.

We are of two minds to them.
Their past and their future
Are lost in our conscious, subconscious.
They have neither. They have both.
What We don't remember, they know.
What We remember, they know.

When the clock began, We were there.
They experienced for us and We for them.

Now it is Time for them
    to re-enter the mainstream of our existence.
     We will be greater for the intimacy.

****

Part VI

ARCTURUS

The Gateway to Earth

Remember We the instant of creation?
Remember We
that moment of dimensional diffusion-confusion?
Remember We the primal directive?
That instant of release becoming chaos complete?
Aloneness? That moment when We exploded
through the pan-dimensional warp?

Some there were who were thrown beyond the abyss,
To gather behind the void
Into scattered cliques of beginningness.
Each group testing the new density and its form.

Arcturans were the ones who reminded themselves
Of seven vibrations below and six above.
Each color-sound having
Twenty-two shades of each step's progression,
With twenty-two others reflecting the minor and more!

Not by chance did they gather into kindred soul groups.
Rather,
        like a magnetic attraction of balanced polarities
            of mate-seeking-mate seeking wholeness,
The thought of co-creating, together, newness, alikeness,
        they joined each other.
And some decided in the flash of creation
        how they would perform their service to All.

Chose they the place in the Universe's warp
Where they could assist us in our epic stories and soul-journs.
Chose they a place that would become
The crossroads, a way-station,
For entry to dimensions and densities to come.

Their home would be a baptismal font
For helping and healing all of our children and futures to be.

They were the Arcturans, the Angelic Host.
The Anubis guides from death to life.
Greeters, some say, waiting in the light tunnel,
Helping souls journey from death's flesh and bones
To new beginnings, if they so chose.

And chose they the Host from the moment of the creation,
To assist all of the beings, kingdoms and realms
Through their private transitions of growth and of form.
Help they the All to grow and become.

It is difficult to explain what it must be
To be alive and yet not with flesh.
Not alive in forms others call life.
Nor can it be expressed in a way lucid and reasonable,
Why they live forever in selfless service,
Seeming to lack wills of their own.
Being neither master nor servant,
They are the gentle comforters to tyrant and slave,
      the rock and the worm.
But "BE" they were and are and beyond death they came,
      to whisper, to nudge and to inspire creation.
For they are the essence of our Creator's heart,
      expressing HIS-HER bliss; The All's divine will.

Make no mistake o' kindred beings,
This does in fact express their free will.

But,
Being different, without density's form and ego,
They live forever and have nothing to prove to you or me.
No karmic challenge to undo, re-do.
No prophetic judgments to make.
Anticipation is all they can do.

They have no galactic webs to unweave.
They are free.... to simply ... enjoy their liberty,
      unfettered by proof of their existence.

They are and always have been
      existing-thriving in their sphere of influence.

Focusing their light energy from the fount of a Good Star,
Remaining always constant and comforting
For the densities above and below.

What say you of those who came forth to be known?
Of Michael, Gabriel, Raphael and Uriel.
Of the sunset's pink glow-love sent by Chamuel
Or the protection of Michael's cleansing fire.
The fresh winds of Raphael,
    the earth of Gabriel and the water of Uriel.
Do they by their presence protect or coerce?
Or are they manifestations of older memories forgotten
    when We, too, were Angels?

****

Now, at the beginning of our co-commitment,
A group of consciousness tarried for a time at Lyra.
They evaluated the show-in-the-making
And decided they to be of service to the greater Galaxy's reality.
They did not feel the need to taste physicality.
Chose they instead to hold on to their enchantment.
Deliberately electing to serve those who would experience flesh,
And live the Law of Separation, the joy of reality.

They are the Angels of mercy and protection,
    assistance and support,
Who bound themselves to the beings of the Worlds.
From the Apex to the Earth. From Lyra to Orion.
From Sirius to the Pleiades.
The Alpha and the Omega of the devic kingdoms
Sought out and attracted themselves
To a place called Arcturus.
    The stargate of the universe.
      Home of the Angels.

So long have they called Arcturus their home
That a million or more stars
    have blossomed and died
In this region of the galaxy.
Transmuting themselves from black to white holes.
Over and over again.
But they, the Angels and their Good Light have remained,

to nourish and nurture, guide and heal,
We, their cousins, who daily live the ordeal.

In concert they decided their future.
They mapped their plan from the beginning.
Establishing a way-station,
A crossroaded rest stop to be called
The Halfway House of the Universe.
Where beings who decided to incarnate physically
 throughout all of the worlds in this area of the galaxy
  would pass through from dimension to dimension,
  from life to death.

Other like-minded cliques
Formed elsewhere to serve other worlds and realities.
The nearest to our knowing is Antares.
Similar in duties, also connected to the Earth,
A counterpart to Arcturus serving other vibrations.

Together the two make a polarized constellation
Spread across the heavens.
Each pulsing different intensities of the primal fire.
Each assuming a unique role.
Each assisting in the reunification
 of all of the beings in the heavens.

And Earth, for the most part, holds close to Arcturus.
Whose energy is compatible with the water-filled flesh,
The oxygen-engorged blood,
 of our mammal-like bodies.

They are the Angels dedicated to serving all of physicality.
It is the role they have given themselves to play
 in the cosmic drama of aliveness.

They are the Angels of service and protection.
Not self-serving like a bullified, bigoted policeman,
 enforcing perfidious laws.
But rather,
Dedicated watcher-helpers for each soul-spark essence
 that walks and talks in the Garden of Trials.

They have made for themselves a vow to mankind:
 To be selfless and loving, supportive and serving,

for EVERY soul's blueprinted life-line trek.
They walk with us, through the good and the sad,
    without wavering.
Savoring
    each moment We create and breathe.
They are literally the extension of ourselves We choose to be,
Day by day, the magnificent mirror of the God we are.

For they are the Guides of the Spirit
    who have been with us since birth.
They are the Angels who have lowered their vibrations
    to be closer to us and the Earth.
They are emissaries of our higher power.
The heaven-sent messengers of The Lords of Time.

Arcturus sends to us the devic kingdom.
The ones who work with the plants and the animals
    and the other creatures of creation.
They are the fairy, the imp, the troll, and the elf.
    So many are their kinds.
        So much is their help.

****

Arcturans are the keepers of the gates
That lead to and from our Earthly bodies.
They monitor the walk-ins of humanity.
Not just the "separate entity" ones,
But also the "soul braiding" kind.

Meaning:
They know the soul's intent,
The blueprint established before our birth.
They were there when it was written.
They wove themselves into our soul-journ roadmap
    because they are a portion of our spirits' guides.

When the body-flesh and mind
Are ready to move forward in time,
To gather new experience-awareness,
And the soul is prompting the movement,
The need for growth is made manifest.
The opportunity is presented and the situation is made ripe.

We, with their help, get set for action.
All that is necessary is the compliance of the will,
The step-aside of the anchoring ego,
And fresh energy enters the flesh
By the epiphany of a knowing.
It travels down the golden cord, connecting our violet crown
To the heavens where all that is ourselves resides,
Leaping over barriers of conditioning and judgment,
Embedding itself into the fertile ground
    of new intelligence, new growth and comfort.

Like plants are We.
No different from the marigold
That withers in the rocky crevices
While flourishing on the loamy terraces.

How did the seed move from place to place?

It was the wind, the bird, the bee, and the storm.
Even man himself made the trip possible.
So it is with all of nature.
Altogether, movement is caused by forces seen and unseen.
No different are you and I
To be unaffected by events swirling around us.
No different the help given without conscious awareness.

This is life.
    And with our lives, We must change.

If conditioning, fear, and resistance is to cause
The restless stirrings of the soul to move forward,
To complete its portion of the plan of reintegration,
The body consciousness finds it is easier to shut down
And say it is something separate, like disease, cancer or stress,
Than to accept that We are much more than walking flesh.

Those who recognize the dis-ease within themselves,
And cease searching for the diet,
    the cure
        and the pill,
Will begin to see
That old habits and patterns of behavior and beliefs,
That glitter without substance or sustenance,

Are preventing our own happiness
and true worth of purpose from unfolding.

Perhaps the cause is too much service to self.
An overabundance of selfishness and paranoia.
Perhaps the cause is too much service to others.
A compelling need to sacrifice and deny self-worth.
When this occurs and you feel "off-track,"
Ask for help, and it shall be given to you
without strings attached.

All that is necessary is for you to open the way,
And they, with your help,
Will infuse your own soul-braiding energy
To dampen or strengthen the will.
To push the body-mind through the veil-wall
that blocks soul's intent from reaching its goal.

Little are the steps taken to preserve a life.
Great is the awareness-making.

And then there are times
when the soul vacates the manifest flesh
And another entity enters the form.
When one leaves and another comes in,
it is done by prior agreement.
The body, the spirit-made-manifest,
needs a different vibration,
compatible with all of the organs and tissues, of course,
yet different just the same.
Like honey in the coffee or carrots in the stew,
To spice the broth, to make the body renew.

It is agreed by both parties and the greater family of man, too,
That the blueprint needs further work before completion.
And the helper-Arcturan agrees to hold the form,
Assisting the healing of the body and the mind.
Keeping the plan moving forward.
While the original entity recovers,
regroups and rests from the trauma or shock
that caused the vacating to occur.

Arcturans have a dedication to our physicality.
They don't need to experience childhood

Or the learning process.
They need to remember their roots.
The beginning of All-That-Is.
They desire to be observers-learners
And to spread light and love.
Obeying the law, assisting the life of all.

And assist they do,
By communication through telepathy and quiet promptings.
By any means possible they communicate.
But mostly through our creativity.

When creative energy is happening,
We open the door-window to Arcturus
        by using our higher energies.
Impulsively We invite in Arcturan influence
        whenever We create.

Dance, art, music, and poetry
All of these are Arcturan in nature.
Their energies are malleable in our reach for genius,
Shapable into anything We aspire.

When our creativity is stumped,
Look to Arcturus and feel the vibration pulsingly pump,
Making an opening in the valve of creation.

Creation itself is an idea
Held fast by the Angels of Arcturus.

When We are creating, We are THE Creator,
As We cohabit with the Creator who is within us.

Arcturus is like a funnel.
The energy passes through its vibration.
Amplified and focused now, its orange-yellow etheric light
Fluxes through Earth's clear, blue, and green chakras,
Beaming balanced, uncluttered thought images and love
        to be grabbed by the asker-user
                and impressed into expression's rush
                        of delightful surprise.

"Did I say that? Did I paint that?"
Wonderment of self-fulfillment rush-flushes the Creator.

Deeply moved is the psyche of the beholder.
And mankind advances a notch.

****

Some feel the Arcturan Angels
And their Antarean counterparts
Are nothing but spiritual elitists.
From that man's point of view, from the bottom of the well,
    they seem "do-gooders" of pious "know-betterness."

If it were true that they avoid physical entrapments,
Just to dodge karma's debt, then it might be true
That they are incomplete in their knowing
And are unable the feel our predicament.
But that judgment is neither accurate nor true,
As their contribution to the plan
    is as grand as any in the Cosmos.

They, like us, are forever enmeshed in the ongoing trilogy.
The reconciliation of Father-Mother God and Me.
Forever working on reunification set forth in the original plan.
To taste separation, to know apartness,
To cry through loneliness, to rage through fear
    caused by ourselves... Together.
They cannot go home without us.
They are as much the tar as We are the baby.

They are our helpmates, through fat and lean.
They weep in frustration
    and suppress tight-jawed indignation
        when small pebbles spread by Chaos
            deflect our attention.

Ongoing, Creation becomes.
The ride of newness keeps the juices flowing.
And goodness-determination guides the prow.
They are the Angels of the Lords and Gods, Ourselves.
More importantly, they are our friends.

Ultimately, everyone and everything understands
Within the very core of its own being
The equality of the Arcturans' vibrations.

And what is the essence of their being?

They hold the vibration of our Creator's Consciousness.
The Arcturans radiate the ray We feel,
   which is,
      Our Creator's Love.

And,
As We near the cusp of Time's time
We will become aware
That We are moving into our own god-hood.
We will glow the golden and sing the pulse
And feel the ecstasy known as Love.
Love for all beings and one another.
And, as We do,
We automatically radiate the Arcturus vibration.

****

Sadly, other pundits would have us believe
   that neither We nor the Angels have free will.

Long, long ago in the ancient days of our world
When jealous gods attempted to manipulate us
And actually tampered with our contribution to the All,
The gods, by their powers and technology,
   distorted our ancestors' knowledge.
Creating the illusion that We were forbidden
   to live our own life as We will.
Oh, what a travesty of devotion this was!

Because
The wheel of karma demands that We live our life freely.
To live the life that We ourselves made and use,
Free to grow and experience.
Free We must be to learn from past mistakes
   and undo the shackles of oppressive beliefs.
To flower in the abundance of opportunities presented.

But the jealous gods would have none of that.
They stripped from our minds our collective memory
And made free choice a sin.
Writing whole books on the mechanics of worship,
They commanded strict obedience of service to themselves.

Ask yourself:

> "Does the God of my book serve His Creator, US,
>   manifesting service to others?
> Or does He serve Himself, assuring service to self?"

If your God is a He, then He cannot serve the We.
There are two parts of polarity. Not one.
One is where We came from. Joined. Combined.
Male and Female. Neither He nor She.
And One is where We are going.
Where, our He-ness will be mated with our She-ness.
Allowing our "We-ness" to hold onto that part of ourselves
    that is joined within our Creator's heart.

This is what the Arcturans make possible for Us.

Look to the mystery that hides on the printed page.
If it is lifeless and guilt-ridden, it screams to be questioned.
Where is service to others? Why just service to self?
Question the arguments and look for completeness.
Seek enlightenment, and it shall be given unto you.

The babel, babels on as all other truth is drowned in denial.

Our fear of offending our "god"
Was gifted to us by a jealous and vain Lyran-Sirian Warlord.
He was not Pleiadian.
Not Arcturan or part of the Founders.
And certainly not our Creator, our Source.
Even so his teachings became rooted
    in the fabric of our mass consciousness.
As he stripped from our being
    the ability to express aberrant behavior
        or even divergent beliefs!
Claiming, "I am the *One God*
    and my followers are the chosen people."

What a guy. What a lie.

For the last five thousand years many of us
Have lock-stepped our way through Time,
Blindly accepting the words of a god
Who would have us believe
That he is the only one who is right,

While ALL of the others are wrong!

Here is the truth:

All truths are part of ALL TRUTH.
Any truth that requires the faithist
To reject other knowledge or beliefs
Is not wisdom, is not WHOLE truth.
It serves no purpose but to keep the believer in darkness.
It violates the Law of Allowance.
It keeps assimilation-reintegration at bay.
It creates "We and They."
Adversaries separated by beliefs, causing wars,
        creating elitist biases,
                driving deeper the stake into the heart of Love,
Shortening Life,
        distorting the Law of One,
                killing the Light.

Blessed are the Arcturans who keep the focus on the plan,
Helping every hu-man become aware of their free will.

Every being,
Every sentient consciousness has free will.
And,
Only those who aren't aware they are free
Insist that only God can be!

What an indictment of Me and Thee!

Lack of free will is a foreign idea.
Birthed in the Constellation of Orion
To live on a world near Sirius.
Exported to Earth by the jealous gods.
They experimented with locking a soul to the plane,
Until the plan was completed.
In desperation they believed
That everyone had to think the same.
And in time the people
Forgot that they were free.

In Orion, the people were denied their free will,
Even in nonphysicality.
Why would they do this to themselves?

Because everyone in Orion knew their source,
    their beginnings,
And they could not hope to think
    that things could be different
        if only they acted more freely.

Apex, Lyra, Vega, and Sirius had taught them this.

Instead they tried to change the structures that bound them.
Not themselves.
They were Apex-like with their "WE-ness"
And knew the dangers of the "I-ness."
They placed all of their power with the group.
Individually this made people frightened of death.
Because
    control within Orion cultures was so deep
        that it was no longer possible for one to escape.
All who tried (they thought) never did.

But that is another topic-epic.
    to be discussed later in Time's continuum.

****

What more needs to said,
About the influence of Arcturus? Of Antares?
Brother and Sister are they,
Like, but unlike Lyra's and Vega's male-female polarity.
One is more of mind and the other is more of the heart.
One is more to guide, the other is more to stimulate.
Together they work for the upliftment of mankind.

It is Arcturus that is assigned
To the Earth's sector of the galaxy.
And it is Antares that is more aligned
With the consciousness of the Andromedan worlds.
Many are the Antareans who incarnate in Andromeda.
Fewer are those who live on the Earth.

Both are the way-stations for nonphysical consciousness
Where We orient-reorient ourselves,
    while moving through our soul-journs.

It is Arcturus that works through the heart chakra feminine.
One-half of the FA tone.

It is Antares that works through the heart chakra masculine.
Bringing the other half of FA to its home.
Like the blue and the red of the flame of a fire,
    they are counterparts to each other.
And together, Fa-Fa creates the music of balance.
Neither one nor the other dominant.
Balanced they are. Integrated they are,
Bringing
    Survival, Sexuality and Power
Together with Communication, Insight and Spirituality.
The tones, the colors,
    Do-Ti, (Red-Violet)
        Re-La, (Orange-Indigo)
            Me-So, (Yellow-Blue)
                Fa-Fa, (Green-Green)
            So-Me, (Blue-Yellow)
        La-Re, (Indigo-Orange)
    and Ti-Do (Violet-Red)
All of the sounds meld in Fa-Fa,
Love's home.
The harmonics of convergence brought forth by the OM.

The mental, focused, scientific,
Data and grid work-oriented Antarean
meets the body sensual, survival-oriented,
Self-expressing Arcturan at the place of integration.
Our own living, beating, pumping heart.
Acting through the left and right halves of the brain.

The magic of the brain to be intuitive
    to leap ahead in awareness
        comes from something divine.
Arcturus is the one that gives us the inspiration.
Antares is the one to structure the conception.
And both feed off each other.

In Earth's past history We were visited by the Lemurians.
Who were densified Arcturans attempting
To live the physical reality.
For a short time it worked.
Their etheric-physical bodies phased
    between seen and unseen by third-density man.

But they lacked the lineal mind
    that would allow them to intensely focus
        and stay on the walk-about Earth-plane.
In time Lemuria dissipated,
    and many remnants of the culture
        repaired to different areas of our planet.
Where large statues were honed from stone
    in tribute to the Brothers from Arcturus.

Easter Island is where physical representations stand
As a silent reminder of their contributions to our world.

And We the Angels have returned,
Guided and protected by Archangel Uriel,
More brave than before to experience
The last Baktun cycles with All That Has Been Created.
Learning to allow all other creation their self-expression.

The Arcturans were present during Atlantean times.
Densifying themselves into that culture.
Making Atlantis a true melting pot of beliefs and peoples.
Beings from many dimensions and realms were there.
And the Arcturans were a part of the play.
Leaving behind the names of the Atlanteans Thoth and Thothme.
Great were their works. Great was their legacy,
Teaching ... transition and change as the culture
Slipped away into oblivion and destruction.
Caused by the conflicts of power
    and the misuse of the energies of the crystal and atom.

The Arcturans were present in ancient Egypt,
Where they densified themselves within the temples.
Taking on the belief systems of the Egyptians
Seemingly to appear as one of their Gods.
Walking among them as Horus and Anubis.
Healing the emotionally ill.
Repairing The Things created by gene-splicing scientists
Seeking slaves to work mindlessly in the quarries
    and the fields of the dimensions below.

We remember Anubis as the one who guides
    individuals to the other side of the veil,
Preparing the spirit to rejoin the soul,

Performing the transition ritual,
Making the journey across the lake,
    a trip to be remembered and savored.

At another time it was the Druids
Who called upon the consciousness matrix of Merlin
To use the gateway of Arcturus
To reached the higher energies of Orion.
Merlin was a bridge between Earth, Arcturus and Orion.

It was during that time
When the earth was falling deeper into darkness,
When the new message of Love
Was being dis-structured by the old Law of Fear,
And the many faces of illumination were being forbidden
    their freedom and liberty to honor their beliefs
        by the conquering Romans and their priests,
That the Druids worked their craft in secrecy.
They remembered their Orion past
    and feared drawing attention to themselves.
Thus feeding their paranoia.

"It is happening again!" They cried.

They knew deep within themselves the pain of death,
    caused by their need to be free.
Revisiting the old habit of secrecy.
They knew that the Priests of the Law
    could find them by their own exaltations.
Their unabashed celebration of Life.

"Suppress emotions!"
    "Be stoic. Deny affection."
        "Live the pain."
            "Give the oppressors nothing to use."
And if found?
    "Die, willingly!"
        "They cannot remove our hearts from the land."

They thought.

They were afraid of attracting attention to themselves.
Hope for the best and expect the worst
    was rooted deep within the Celtic mentality.

But they remembered Merlin,
    who had helped them before on Orion.
And by Merlin they reached Arcturus.
To touch the future potential of themselves.
To manifest the healing that Arcturus could bring.

The Druids knew that the Wicca they used
Allowed Merlin to access Arcturus.
As Avalon dissipated, Merlin sparked,
As Orion the negative rubbed against Arcturus the positive.
And great works were done
    as Arcturus protected the people
        from the darkness besetting them.

Many more are the examples of Arcturus who
Together with Sirius, The Dog Star, White Wolf,
Has helped the people of Earth.
Providing healing energies for the sexually abused,
    the tormented and troubled.
Providing the means to heal
    by calling in the loving embrace of the Creator
Who watches over All That Is.

Subtle is the Arcturan influence
To use their energies when We are awake.
Blatant is their work when We are tired or in dream state.

The great ones who come while We are asleep,
Making adjustments to the spine and neck,
Touching the organs that need assistance,
Leaving us refreshed and fulfilled,
    are the same ones who helped our ancestors.

Gather they the forces necessary
To comfort and heal the body, mind and spirit
Whenever the call for help is sent.
From the beginning of time they have responded,
Never once complaining: "Not now."

Arcturus is a mirror that allows us to see
The positive and negative halves of ourselves.
Just as our pets, the animals, do.
This is a translation of Arcturan energy
When it interacts between our animal friends and ourselves.

When We act with Arcturus
We attract positive energy to ourselves.
We make a moment of stillness and breathe through the heart,
allowing
    its nurturing calmness to cleanse
        all parts of our psyche and self.

And,
When a baby is born and the consciousness
    propels itself through the dimensions,
        the womb, the tunnel, toward the Earth plane,
It stops at Arcturus to gather its strength.

It is here that the spirit is prepared
For the soul-journ's Earth-plane experience.
The process of selecting the parents is solidified.
The sex is chosen ... not always at the moment of conception
    as our disfocused priest-scientists would have us believe,
        but sometimes at the moment of birth,
            when the death we call life begins.
Chromosomes X and Y dance in flux,
    awaiting the spirit's whim.

The Arcturans work with the preborn
Solidifying the agreement it is about to live.
It will help the new one to choose
Between closing or opening the veil,
Allowing or preventing past-memory bleed-through.
The reward and punishment of both edges of this sword
    are understood completely before birth.

They assist in the formulation of the life's blueprint,
Making the Arcturus energy more involved
In the new life's expression.
Helping prepare the script,
Being supportive during the transitional decisions
That will be faced throughout the life experience.
They provide a state of balance for the spirit
    before it enters the traumatic transition of birth.

And when the life called
    "The Walk through the Valley
        of the Shadow of Death" is complete,

And the individual leaves the Earth Plane,
One of the first stops it makes is Arcturus.

Those who survive the Near-Death Experience
Report seeing a light at the end of the tunnel.
The light is not the star of Arcturus but rather
The vibration of its consciousness.
Which means to some, the Christed One.
Others say it is God, Nirvana, The Buddha,
    or a loving relative or friend.
The energy of Arcturus is all of that.
The senses cannot describe bliss beyond bliss,
    unlimited happiness.
It must have a name
And they express it as the Comforter.
And the light is the vibration of Arcturus.

It is the Arcturans who heal and nurture
All who have met traumatic deaths.
Whether by mass agreements of wars and disease.
Or one-at-a-time life-ending decisions.
They comfort all who walk in the Valley of Death.
Suicide, genocide, wars, or AIDS.
The cause is not judged.
The spirit needs only to embrace the reason.

Is it not clear that the birth and the death processes are the same?
Birth has the biological tunnel with the light at the end.
Death is a dimensional tunnel with a light at the end.
It is the same because all of existence is a cycle.
It is the nature of the Universe to respect its own rhythm.

The Arcturans continually manifest
Emotional and sexual healing.
Their energy heals the abused children
And helps them retain their sense-of-wellness-being.

Without knowing why, the children are healed.
Because,
    for them,
        they are players in the molesters' trauma and pain.
Making small steps toward the conclusion
    of the polarity-balancing game.

101

The game.

Like a conch shell cycling tighter and tighter upon itself,
It continues to roll toward its sweet beginning.
And it will be.

The ram's horn trumpet of Gabriel that will sound
The note of the final completion.
Celebrating, as did Joshua,
    the destruction
        of the walls of our prison.

****

Part VII

The Elders Of Sirius

And the fragments scattered throughout the Is-ness,
Group Consciousness,
    Families of Consciousness,
        Individual Consciousness,
           The Founders
                and the Angels of Arcturus-Antares,
All allowed themselves to be attracted
    to different areas of the Universe.
Leading the way for the refugees and pilgrims
    fleeing the wars of mind and bomb.

It has been written
That when the We had come through the prism,
Some of us had stopped at Lyra and thought,
    "We don't need much reintegration.
        We don't have many lessons to learn.
           Let us just rest here at Lyra and Vega
           and watch the rest of the show go by."

But in time some of our We-ness had allowed themselves
To be sucked into Lyra's feminine realities.
Or into the Vegan masculine contrariness.

They, a great portion of our We,
Began to form judgments.
They began to believe
That only *they* knew the way to lead us back home.
And
Without trying,
Many of our Brothers and Sisters found themselves
Totally enmeshed in the conflict.
And by so doing they sliced a rift between Lyra and Vega.

Another portion resisted the temptation
And in sorrow moved away from the race-driven drivel,
The arrogant strutting,
That was perverting the work of ourselves and the Founders.

They left the prism of Lyra and its newly made prison
Of cultivated, culture-aided biases
In search of an alignment of great Sols
That would by themselves assist in balancing
The arrogant piety that was destroying
    all of the known worlds of our youth.

They followed the Founders' trail like quail
    plucking bread crumbs from the floor of the forest.
Ever more in awe of the greatness of these beings,
Who, by their focus on our Creator's loving admonition,
    "Think of another way to be,"
Created platforms and stages infinite
Where the play so serious could be limitless
    in its ways and vistas unknown.

They found a clearing ringed all about
    by the glistening tear drops of a great constellation.
On the edge of a galaxy milky-white with light,
They found the three great furnaces of Sirius,
Glowing, pulsing the harmonics of tones so divine
That they caused
The newly forming planets and realms to show
    matter, mind and spirit
        so perfectly-blissfully unified-aligned in their orbits
As to create an opera of such drama
That it would leave the collective heavenly host
    breathless and exhausted,
        thrilled and stunned,
By the multitudinous probable realities that would flow
From its trinary star grouping.
So balanced in the ways of nature's perfection they were.

Showing by heat-fire, song and light,
Visible to the walk-abouts,
    creepy-crawlies
        and water-borne creatures,
That this place would be the holiest of holies,
The grandest of the grandness,
Most perfect of all of the outdoor stadium-cathedrals
Thus far set aside for our great experiment to try.

Where the making of our, We The Angels', future,
would-could be seeded and assured.

Sirius became the nursery of our universe.
Where planets were set aside exclusively for cats, or crystals,
or horses, wolf-dogs and whales,
or man-forms and ferns,
or corn and flowers scented so sweet
they would assail the senses,
disrupting self-indulging thoughts,
causing even the most swallowed-up intellect
to stop and think
about the grandness of the plan We live within.

It would only be a matter of time.

****

A portion of the Is-ness, now voyagers of Time,
stopped their migration at Sirius and thought:

"We feel this place will serve our purpose.
We see three stars aligned to cause growth,
out from
and toward
balance and unity.
No matter the reality that would be brought to this place,
the place itself would make it impossible
for the idea to remain unchanged."

Satisfied, they became the Elders of Sirius.
And here they tarried for an eternity.

They had seen that the Lyra-Vega conflict
Would continue to escalate in its self-righteous assertions.
That the nonphysical Lyran-feminine nurturer
would mince about the air
distaining to dip into physical flesh,
Choosing instead to bombard those who lived
Within the manoid vessels of skin and hair,
With visions of goodness, light and love.
Overruling self-determination.
Distorting the left-hand path of the Law of One.
Creating victims ripe for domination.

Saw they that the male-assertive Vegans
Would push at their borders and boundaries.
Expanding their supremacy.
Developing deliciously efficient ships
Of space travel and war-making.
Driving the physical Lyrans from their homelands and realms.
Conquering,
     polluting
          even the Apex experiment,
Causing the Founder-based plan to go crookedly and die
In the self-indulgent cul-de-sacs found while traveling
     the right-hand distortion of the Law of One.

It became only a matter of time before the conflict-makers
Would move away from Lyra-Vega into the vast
     surrounding realms of other newness
          and encounter the great star system of Sirius.
Where their explorers and scouts would find
     worlds and realms prepared by the great ones,
          the Elders of Sirius.
The spirits and beings of Lyra-Vega would find
     the nonphysical God-Parents
          of a billion worlds and creatures to come.

They would find that while
They had worked through the bile
     of the first,
          second,
               and third trials of unity,
Others had, by their own efforts,
Followed the Founders' example of seeding
And had become
     the first etheric
          and genetic
               engineers of the Universe.

Long before the Apex was a thought considered
     by the Founders, the Elders began.

We mean:
Instead of seeding their genetics directly
Into the indigenous species

That were growing and becoming
On the worlds of the stars that allowed them to stay;
And then jumping into their newly made expression
When everything was ripe for co-creation, they waited.
Saying the Word that would be heard
Throughout the Universe:

> *"Ready are these creatures.*
> *For themselves they are ready.*
> *Imbued with the nourishment of like-begets-like,*
> *self-becoming more like the source that We came from,*
> *they are prepared.*

> *"As in the creation of the likeness of ourselves,*
> *they will become the mind-traps of our Creator itself.*
> *And will*
> *by our grace and continence*
> *live forever."*

The Elders would prepare the worlds for the arrival
  of the Lyra-Vegan positive and negative moths and bees
    that would be attracted to Sirius' pollen-rich,
      balanced flame.

Desiring that Sirius A and B be
The first colonized star bases,
And holding Sirius C reserved for later drama,
They set about infusing their energy
Into the solid matter that was forming
  throughout the third-density worlds of the three suns.

Their goal was to create compatible vessels
For the higher frequency vibrations of the great souls
  that would be migrating from Lyra and Vega.
They created-prepared, too, the nonphysical realms
For the consciousness that would remain etheric.

As the conflicts in Lyra and Vega warmed uncomfortably,
Probes came more frequently to the Sirius worlds.
Scouts found places equally suitable
For both the negative and positive ideals.

The Elders had prepared their worlds with meticulous care,
Knowing completely

that the conflict would spread like a virus,
Engulfing and changing their paradise before moving on.
It would be their mission to amplify
The Founders' primal codings to resolve
The challenge of reintegration.

And they knew that the differences
Between the Lyrans and the Vegans
 would pollute the minds of gods and man,
Driving them further apart.
Until one day
When the moon would turn blue,
 and the sun would stand still,
Gods and man would see their creator-selves' images
In the mirror that does not lie and say,
 "You are us."

But that day would be reserved for a future solstice of winter.
When the worlds would sleep,
Tired and long exhausted by the busy entrapments
 of the creatures who think
 and act contrary to their needs.

****

And the Lyran and Vegan disappointed no one.
Except maybe themselves.

Exactly as anticipated by the Elders of Sirius
They began to arrive,
 freshly discouraged by their efforts,
To unify the Law of One.
Leaving their established worlds solidified and stuck
In their plans of differences and apartness.
Driving wedges between the Brothers and Sisters.
Ending with chaos complete at the Apex.

Rememberest thou,
That the Founders had fragmented themselves
Throughout all of the universes?
Spreading-embedding themselves
Into everything that ever was and ever will be?

Rememberest thou,
The stargated way-stations that had been established,
Forever guaranteeing sanctuaries and rest havens
For the weary soul and star-traveler?

Remember We,
The plan of all that was,
Was to grow out of our epic soul-journ
A means to escape our self-made prison?

Co-creationists are We.
    Remember?

If you do, then you will recall
That We The Angels of All That Is
Moved away from the prism of our birth
Into the trinary star system of Sirius.
Where two are seen as one orange-yellow, blue-red spotlight
Shining as a beacon in the Earth's dark sky.
While the third warms the hearth of our world.

And so it was that the home worlds of the Elders
Were reached first by the battle-weary Vegans.
The strong, strutting, masculine specimens
    of consciousness warriors.
They brought all of their glorious assertionary airs
To a pastoral world that could soothe their embattled spirits.
They chose the Helios Sun to make their home.
By thought and by ship they moved
A greater portion of their species and forms
From their war-torn homes in the stars,
To this new land that shone
So promisingly beacon-like in their eyes.

Fresh from the (sick)cess
Of their genetic manipulation of the bipedal mammals
On their own home planets in Vega,
The newly arrived dove headlong into bringing the emerging,
    Elder-prepared Two-Legged Sirian up to their standards
        of paranoia and intellect.

They would reaffirm
All of future humanity's deep-rooted need

To manipulate indigenous third-density genetics
In order to accelerate their own development.
And thus, by using the host
Already imbued with the Founders' and Elders' programs,
They hastened their own return to the Source.

With them too they brought their need for dominance
Which could only be perpetuated in solid-sentient form.

And, at the same time, they collectively elected
To close the veil on their past existence
So that they could emerge-merge into their new home,
With a consciousness lacking an awareness of their history.
Thinking: If they knew not their past,
       they would not walk the same path.

So tightly structured had they made
The Sirian-man's genetic memory,
That they had lost their divine knowledge of who they were!

Sound Familiar?

Another truth was born in Sirius:

> *"As above, so below.*
> *All cycles need to repeat,*
> *until they are complete."*

But they, in their passion to hurry through the plan,
Birthed themselves with a veil so dense,
A cloak so opaque,
They were destined to repeat the same mistakes.
The difference being that this time
The created being would not know why,
And in so doing bring greater knowing
To a higher level of understanding that is waiting for us
      in this, the last Baktun.

The trouble was that only one point of view
Was frozen into the mind of the hapless vehicle.
No thought was given to the idea
That the second distortion of the Law of One
Could be so self-serving, its focus so skewed,
That it would cause one liberty after another
To be stripped from their being.

The being that would be called the negative Sirian
    did not dream.
They did not bother to investigate the inner part of themselves
That craved expression for creation.
They had no need to be different.
Instead,
    all they sought
        was to dominate.

They expanded the basic animal trait to establish territory.
To exploit, to conquer, to wax greatly in order to bathe
    in the adoration of their fellow-man.
For they were men.
Different in appearance from us,
    but bipedal walk-abouts just the same,
Packing a gun and asserting themselves
    upon anything that stood in their way.

This was the existence they called life.
It was all they allowed themselves to know.
How far had they fallen, compared to everything We know?
How far are they from us?

They would be the deranged grizzly in the field of deer.
Killing without eating, just for pleasure.

Sound familiar?

For us they were the first
To test every category of zealous domination.
By their own will, they drank the swill of their past
And refused to process it.
Keeping it contained and strangled within,
    without knowing it was a bitter poison
        that was destined to annihilate them.
In the interim its bitterness kept them alive,
    for they hadn't allowed themselves to know better.
They took their idea and stretched it
    to the greatest extreme
        that the Sirius-being
           could offer.

And into this illusion of dominating their environment
And controlling their evolution
Came the Lyrans with their message of light and salvation.
  "Follow me, I know the way,"
    was being expressed another way.

These first Lyran pilgrims chose to remain
    nonphysical fourth-, fifth- and sixth-density beings.
They came seeking a place where they could escape
From the war and dis-structure
That had torn their home worlds apart.

Chaos had tested the Law of One
And had won
    a short-lived victory.
Expelling the Lyrans who could not abide
The disintegration of their homelands,
Chaos forced these etheric beings to leave,
Compelling them to find other untested ideas
Residing in the sand-box of the Universe.

And the fertile ground that was Sirius
Lay waiting for the curious to mouse out the cat.
Where the philosophical and cultural differences
Of our Lyran-Vegan grandparents
Would influence our future's physical development.
Where warriors would be tough.
And intellectuals would be soft.
Where the pendulum swings of right and wrong
    would swing to and fro,
        hopefully not as violent as before.

****

Lyra had thought,
    "Let us attract ourselves to a portion of the universe
        where we can work out our ideas
            and get back home."

And they had reached out and found Sirius.
The Dog Star of Orion, The Serpent of the Garden.

And so the conflict came to balanced Sirius.
And the game became a notch more serious.

Sirius was always and always will be a trinary star group.
With a perfect triangle there are always two polarities opposed,
Balancing the third equal-distant, the joined part of ourselves.
Two-dimensional space sees the three separate dots
    as the primary matrix of unity, stability.
Three-dimensional space sees tetrahedral GEMS
        comprised of four sides (races),
            with four points (seasons)
        and six edges (epochical days) to experience.
To rest in the seventh most perfect sphere they create.

No matter which three you see,
    there is always a fourth to know.

And so
Lyra and Vega brought two parts of ourselves
Together, making the geometric tetrahedron to Sirius.
To live again the goal of reintegration,
That grew exponentially throughout Orion's constellation.
All separated by a gap, the ego,
    known as the Abyss,
        polarized apart,
            waiting for the joining of its parts.

The Lyrans traveled to the Sirian star group.
Where they found
A nonphysical fifth-density dimension
    that they could exist in.

At first the Lyrans stayed apart from the Vegans.
Hovering about in the nonphysical planes,
Opting to remain in this plateau of awareness
Attempting to influence lower-density minds
    with clearer thought
        and messages of spiritual awareness.

The Vegan-Sirians could not hear, feel or see
The efforts of their Lyran Sisters.
So total was their self-made exile.
They did not see, nor understand,
The closed, looped road they were walking.
And the Lyrans didn't understand the Vegans' need
To experience this form of separation.

But someone had to take this path
   and live it to its fullest extreme,
      else it would be left to you and me
         or some other person to try.
No idea could be left unheeded.

And the Elders watched
   as the Lyrans transmuted their energy
      into third-density matter and mind.

For the Lyrans saw that the Vegan-Sirians had become
Emotionally and physically ill
From their lives of dominance and control.
Ulcers and cancers ate at the flesh and bones
Of this tightly focused man-species
And the Lyrans became concerned.

In all fairness, in a good way, the Lyrans had sought to help.
Not by tampering with the genetics that were already in place.
Not by seeking to incarnate themselves
   and walk amongst the people preaching
A totally alien message of salvation and integration.
They knew full well the future of that.

Instead they placed their energies
Into the foods the people would eat,
Into the metals that would make ships and guns,
Into the stones that would build great cities,
And into the very subconsciousness of the beings' minds
   that could not discern
      where this increased pain and discomfort came from.
The results were completely contrary to their efforts.

The Lyrans caused more violent behavior
And tension-manifested disease of such excruciating levels
That the Elders themselves had to intercede.

Spoke Helios and Vesta and the others:

> *"Great ones of Neberu in Lyra!*
> *Glorious are the deeds you have done.*
> *Wondrous the works you have accomplished.*
> *Stop now and look at what has become of your efforts.*
> *The people bleed from unknown sores.*

Their essence is dissipated keeping their planned focus.
It is by their efforts to live out aggression in all its forms
that We may return to our Source.
Leaving us to try other paths of existence.

"We desire peace for all of creation.

"Would you deny the seed to grow and bear its fruit,
no matter how bitter its meat?
We see that you would not.
Nor would the Hunters
you are attempting to change
allow you to become nothing more than their slaves.
You and those who are still coming
from our beginning place
desire to help others
by nurturing and healing.

"So be it.

"From Sirius let the scorching one
take the misery and pain
from THOSE WHO ASK! O Great Ones!
FROM THOSE WHO SEEK RELIEF AND HELP
AND ANSWERS HIDDEN
BY THEIR CULTURE AND LEADERS.

"We say now,
before this idea ends in failure and death
exactly as it did before,
Stop your interference now!
The great harmonics of our Elysian star matrices
and the beings that live on its planets
cannot abide your interference.
You and those who wish to continue this conflict
must take it somewhere else,
away from the influence of these three great Sols
whose sole purpose is to show the way of harmony.
Living TOGETHER
and ALLOWING
each to be their own sovereign.

"Those who feel they need to live their lives entrapped
in the mindless pursuit of self-aggrandizement,

> *without the need of spiritual enlightenment,*
> *may remain bathed by the harmonics of the star that cleanses.*
> *One day they shall emerge from their self-made prison.*
> *Just as you will from yours."*

Thus spake the Elders of Sirius.
And they by their knowledge of the Space and Time
Found a home for the Vegan-Lyran conflict in Orion.
Thus, the Dog of Sirius leads the way for the Hunter.

It was not a banishment.
For the Hunters did not know what had occurred
And therefore could not know their future had been changed.
Where once these early Vegan refugees might have died
From the Lyran-caused disrupture
    of the trinary star system's harmonics,
Making the Vegan plan of spiritual denial
    and total selfishness
        to wither and end,
The Elders had given the Vegan people,
Who would continue to leave their home worlds, a choice:
    Come to Sirius
        or go to Orion.

In Sirius they would be quarantined
To live out the plan's time, left alone.
In Orion the full magnitude of the conflict
Between the two great cultures
Would be played out in a place more suitable
To the dynamic tension between them.

Sirius was to be a healing place,
Where the three stars would facilitate movement
    from both extremes toward the middle integration point,
        without external interference!
Except, of course,
    for the harmonics of the stars and planets themselves.
These beings, by themselves, co-create us.

It was established by the Elders that in Sirius,
The positive and negative would live apart
    until they grew together.

Orion would allow the Lyran idea of service to others
To penetrate the shields of the mind of the Hunter
In a more compatible electromagnetic pulse-light.
They could now be left alone to work out their own
    final, final destiny.

Helios and Vesta saw that Orion
Was the phantom fourth point of the GEM tetrahedron,
Formed by the stars placed by Chaos
    to show unity juxtaposed.

****

And so it was.

A long time ago the future looked both bright and grim.
Flailing about,
    turning pages of the ancient books of wisdom,
Frantic to find solutions and answers to the simple question:
"How do We get back home?"
Our ancestors, who were both angels and men,
Pushed, pulled, prodded, and changed the course of history
    with each breath and thought.

Fluid is the flux of thought.
Powdery are the explosive sparks of action.
Realities were cast out upon the universe,
    like so much garbage from the bow of a ship.
We did not realize that the offal was not biodegradable.
Its half-life was Carnotian in its collapsing cycles.
Feeding upon itself, by changing words and deeds small,
    minuscule half-step advances towards our collective goal.

Gods that We are,
The realities We make cannot be left unfinished.
Nor can they be left undone.
All things vibrate to a pulse,
symbolic of the in-and-out breath
    of our Living, Loving Creator.

And so it is.

As above, so below. We live forever.
Only the lifetimes change.

There is no escaping our thoughts and actions.
The Law of Karma assures us of that.

If We interfere in this lifetime,
We will be interfered with by the very ones We help or hurt
   the next time We have a lifetime together.

And so it was
That the negative Sirian civilizations were left intact.
And the people's minds, still tightly cloaked
   behind their veil of spiritual denial,
Would cycle through many lifetimes to come,
Not knowing that they could move to Orion
To re-enter the wars of good and bad.
Some did, of course, having come to the conclusion
That something was wrong with their lives.
But this awareness was not quickly learned.

It would be left to the soul itself
To keep prompting the spirit-made-manifest,
That something was missing, something was wrong.
The very soul that they denied existed
Was the means to move them
Out of their flesh-locked incarnation cycles.
And they left ... one by one ... for Orion.

So complex are the ideas of Allowance,
Freedom of Expression, and Liberty
That zones had to be established
Where one or the other or all could be lived
Apart for awhile
   until the mass consciousness
      clamored for change.

Sirius would be a healing place, birthing ideas,
And would resist being rent asunder by the conflicts created.
Even so,
The Elders would have their work disrupted time and again,
Having to find places more suitable
   for the dynamics presented to fight over.
They did not play the possession game.
Nothing in Sirius was owned by one culture or the other.
All belonged to all and they would protect

The balance of these stars from the disruptions
That postured and pranced in their midst.

They became the translocators of conflict
If it waxed as great as the one
The Vegan-Hunter had experienced.
They reserved Sirius as the integration point.
The home of our future selves,
The place that We will migrate through
     on our return to our very first home.

Complicated the plan.
Headstrong the magistrates.
But as long as it served the purpose of perpetuating
The need for All That Is to experience All That Is,
Their Will
     will be done.

And so the conflict moved to Orion
Where it could exist in isolation, uninterrupted.
Interfered with, yes. But not interrupted.
This great war of wills had to be played to its grievous end.
And the stars that were chosen suited this need.

For some of the Lyran wannabe gods (not all)
a lesson was learned.
Don't interfere with any plan.
Better to leave it be than attempt to change another
     before the other desires to change.

An idea of the Elders was introduced to the Lyrans,
     and the Lyran-Sirians began to change.

****

Now that the conflict had been safely moved to Orion
Each side began to assimilate the Sirius consciousness.
The Law of Environment began to control,
Just as it was planned by the Elders.
A code embedded as deep as the Founders' fragments
was rising up to be felt and be heard.

No matter where you are in the Universe,
Nor how foreign the place may be to you,

The planets and stars will change your vibration.
You will adapt or you will die or be driven away.

And so it was
That a sizable portion of the original Vegans and Lyrans
Had found their home in Sirius.
Different as cat and dog,
    shark and dolphin,
        dragonfly and butterfly,
            man and woman were they.
They were invited by the Elders to stay
And work through their differences of life-making.
Knowing that in time, the harmony of the place
    would allow them both to grow out of their tendency
        to interfere with others in a good or a bad way.
Pushing them to recognize that their kindred differences
Were just an idea, divided by itself.

Here in Sirius, We learned that
The spirituality-denying Vegans would be known
For their outrageous ways
    and their incredible self-centeredness.
Much like the Emperors of Orion they were.
But much more secretive.
Displaying paranoia and treachery that would cause
The cruelest despot of any world
    to blanch and hurl his lunch.
They served only themselves,
    not an idea, nor an Empire.

From the beginning of their history
There never has been a parade of victory,
Medals of honor or adulation pinned on any hero's chest.
GOD FORBID (if they ever knew of such a deity)!
That would have been his or her certain death.
No one person ever rose to be king or queen.
No one ever vowed their allegiance to another. Ever.

In this society to be an old person
Was both a sign of weakness and strength.
Either they were battle-honed clever
    or they were cowards.
It didn't matter to the marauding band of Vikings

That would stumble upon the villages of separate tents.
First they would seek out and kill the old ones
    and then the children.
All the while the village would be killing the invaders.
Making the war much more pleasurable to all.

If the strangers succeeded in winning,
They would take the surviving women and young men
For sport pleasure in ways that cannot be described.

Humiliation was the goal.
Then death.
Never compassionate-magnanimous actions
    meant to win the hearts of the conquered.
Suicide might have been an option to the survivors,
    if ever it had occurred to them. But it didn't.
In a sado-masochistic way they took upon themselves
    the most brutal kinds of torture
        and then carried the exquisite pain to their graves.
Never to be known by anyone but themselves.
That was their hero's way.

They were the berserkers and dark-arts magicians,
Cunning usurpers of everyone's liberty.
These were the negative Sirians.

And the Lyrans-Sirians, the positive ones,
Would become the healers and nurturers,
    the great illuminators of humanity.
        Warriors of another kind.
Who by their own abilities to alter genetics,
Became long-lived and incredibly wise
In the art of diplomacy and social matters.
They invented great machines of health,
Commerce and of war.
Becoming game-warden-like,
Monitoring the movements and evolution of the Self-Heroes,
The Vegan-spawned Sirians.
Who needed desperately to be watched and contained.

They would from time to time,
An age or two apart,
Drop in on their mindless, more savage neighbor

And subvert the plot of a dastardly War-Lord
That might have blossomed
Into the complete eradication of a planet.

But this they did less and less frequently,
    deciding instead
To shut off their enemy from the ethers of space.
Preventing their peculiar cancer from spreading
Beyond the borders that the Elders had said
Were this aberration of existence's home.

More frequently there were clashes with their Lyran Brothers
Who just couldn't overcome their own nature to interfere
In the natural order of things beyond their control.
These Lyrans could not allow
The Brutal Ones they called "The Evil"
    the opportunity to grow
        out of their mind-trap of unawareness.

Blustered the Lyrans,

    "How much more pain would they give, when they learn
    of the Plan? Wouldn't they be angry to think that they
    were denied their minds of consciousness-awareness?

            "Kill them now! Be done with them.
            Nothing good ever came from Vega."

The wise Lyrans, now Sirians, had grown up.
Less like their Lyran forefathers, more purely Sirian.
They actually protected the Vegan-Spawn from annihilation.

Thus the negative and positive of Sirius was firmly defined.
And the Elders watched with some apprehension,
Knowing that both polarities would change.
Slowly, one generation-step after another they would change,
Because the adversaries had called Sirius their home
    and they could not change the Stars.

****

Part VIII

ORION

The Three Phases of Darkness

Twilight

And so the desperate war of the gods
Fell from the heavens and landed in Orion.
Banished to a sector of the galaxy to flail in rage,
While being shackled by their irons of piety and control.

When We were in unity with the whole
And conscious that We were "All That Is,"
We decided to experience maximum separation
And fragmented ourselves into billions of pieces.

We entered the reality of the Triad,
The specific template comprised
Of one polarity and its opposite,
    and the need to recombine the two.

Millions of years later the conflict moved
From Lyra and Vega and lived for a spate in Sirius.
And then,
When
    the disruption become too intense
        for the Alpha and Beta healers to abide,
The emulation was exiled to Orion
    to be closer to the great red giant star
        called Betelgeuse.

The electromagnetic pulses of discomfort,
Felt by all beings near Bat-al-juaza,
Are the reason the conflict continued to grow.
This great one floods the entire Shoulder of Orion
With a vibration that is excruciating
To the inner guts and juices
Of all who call this area their home.

Its job is to cause the self to battle itself
And forces the conflict to continue.

The Elders of Sirius said:

> "*It will be left to the great one to resolve
> the most intense portions of hu-man differences.*"

It would be left to Orion to be
The final battle ground of maximum polarity.
Where the widest of differences between
Service to self and service to others
Would be confined from time before time until now.

Beginning with emotional conflicts within their society,
Expanding to make
    a whole galaxy of political beasts
Who would, by their need to maintain their positions,
Corrupt all of their inner knowings and beliefs.

For all of Orion knew their past,
Not like the Vegan-Sirians who had shut down their minds
And suffered more completely our need to be ignorant.
Orion gives us a glimpse of our most concrete example
    of alternate reality-making and playing.
One that We would not have to repeat on Earth.

Orion's history is written in the Oahspe;
It is whispered of in the Urantia;
It is hinted about in the Torah;
And is explored in the movies of the imagination.

It is the place where spiritual denial manifested:
Service to self's domination and
Service to others, subservience, submission.
It is the place where the dominators used and abused
    the less aggressive ones
        and actually controlled their wills!

By sorcery and black magic, hexes and spells,
They bombarded each other with curses and terror.
Causing the people to shut down their emotions
Fearing that they would be exposed for being ... happy!

Heaven forbid that should occur.

Blessed were the controllers who would not allow
  bliss and goodness to be.
Blessed were the elite
  who would stand on the necks of the meek,
    grinding them further into their vow of humility.
Blessed was the Empire
  that would break up love bonds and marriages,
    changing the supplicant's work,
      making sure it was something disliked.
Blessed were the Majordomos
  who would transfer their workers
    to another continent or planet
      to prevent friendships from ever occurring.
Blessed was the stake of bitterness
  that killed the heart of Hope,
    shunting the passion of life,
      eradicating the need to imagine
        something better for themselves and their children!
Blessed was everything
  that forced everyone
    to submit to control.

The Empire.
Their control over everything social was strictly monitored
As family sizes were rigidly fixed
To keep the numbers of daughters and sons,
Aunts and uncles and cousins, to the minimum few.
Keeping blood bonds limited and the village of relatives
Diluted in the great city-states of slaves.
Preventing wars of the clans from occurring.

This was the daily life of the Orion.
Tightly focused.
Not blinking, as murder, intrigue and molecular manipulation
  ran rampant throughout the community.

So tight was the focus of their polarity
That Freedom, Liberty and Justice for all
Were never thought to be rights of the individuals.
The state provided their citizens with everything,
Including the body for their next incarnation.

The soul became less and less instrumental
In the birth-and-death process of the citizen.
Creating more and more stress on the spirit.
And in time the people became trapped
In the cycle of flesh to death to flesh,
Unable to discern what it meant to know
        the illusion that all of creation calls life.

They could not escape from the unending rounds
        of role playing, mayhem and spiritual denial.
And it would be ages before they would discover
From the depths of their despair
A bridge that was to be called Merlin.
The wizard of action tapped by the Wicca,
        discovered by the Masters of Silence.

Alas, however, this would not happen
Until the soul of the people screamed,
        "This existence cannot continue!"

For you see,
In the beginning the souls, after death,
Would switch sides,
Rebirthing in the house of their opposites,
        trying to find a solution to the struggle.

In the end
Even this demonstration of free will was blocked,
As the caste system of Orion was birthed.
Similar to the models here on the Earth.
But with one major difference.

In Orion it wasn't a belief, playing with the cycles of karma,
And the need to walk a mile in another's shoes,
It was a reality based on rewards of duty to the state.
Where power begat more power.
And misery fell further from grace.

Control over all things played back and forth,
Always reminding the subservient ones
That in order to serve the whole,
They needed to give up the self.
You know the feeling. The hang-headed one

When you are shamed to walk a line of obedience
Instead of living your life of beingness.

Control was the Empire's game.
Even the thoughts of the people were monitored
And telepathic communication was not allowed to be.
The people were able to think-talk, you see,
Like all of our Animal Brothers can do.
Like all of the Apexian, Lyrans, Vegans and Angels can do.
But the Empire used the intense discomfort
Of the Red-Giant Star to scatter the thoughts,
And with high-intensity disruptors-generators,
They caused waved floods of ultrasonics to be heard and felt,
Making thinking privately an ear-bloody,
    mind-puddling experience.
The pain caused cancer of the brain.
The body craved to shut down.
As the Empire maintained its control.

We speak of the ancient times of Orion
When escape was never an option,
When each philosophy was fresh in its belief
That the other would give a quarter
    and join them on the middle road to home.

HA! Unlike the fantasy of the toad and the princess,
The kiss would not happen for a millennium or more.
The red giant Betelgeuse would assure them of this.

****

Midnight

In the beginning,
Before the cultures were strutting their technological stuff,
There was a mutual agreement between slave and master
To hold close to their rigid, steel-strapped, societal structures.
But as the history of sameness progressed,
The state's control became even more tightly clinched.
Preventing all individuals from escaping after death.
No one could leave the oppression of the state.
No one was free from the Empire's grip.

Our cellular memory remembers the conflict.
Our books of fantasy and space replay its control.
Conflict is rooted
Within the very core of every being of the humanoid race.
Not one culture on the face of the earth
Is free of the nightmare of domination and fear
That rages mythically in their dreamstate minds!

In Orion it was dangerous to dream.
"Big Brother is watching" was a fact in this garden of horror.
The citizen had to control all his thoughts and musings,
For fear that the "Correctors of Behavior"
And the "Monitors of Dreams" would swoop down
        and remove his mind altogether.
Using shock, chemicals and magic to destroy
The root cells of reason and memory.

For you see, in your dreams you travel
        and meet other dreamers along the way.
And they, with you, work through
        your combined hopes, dreams, and wishes.
A dangerous place to be caught by the watchers
        who sleep-walk the roads of despair.

How long would it be, then, We would wonder,
Before the Founders would intercede,
Releasing the Empire's control?
How long would the injustice continue to hold
        everyone a slave to their self-made prison?
When would the Orion begin to change?

The Founders and the Elders of Sirius knew
        that Orion was meant to be an aberration.
A reality created by the Lords of Darkness and Light
Who kept the Emperors asserting their dominance
        and their subjects from loving their life.
The Founders were not going to interfere.
Because, there were only two options available.
And both were up to the Orions.
Either they would destroy themselves
And the idea would be repeated elsewhere,
Or

they would evolve
    and become aware of their godhood.

The Founders and the Elders
Would have to wait for the people to awaken
And make known their desire for change.
Until that time the Universe would hold its breath
    and wait for the spark to occur.

And it did in a way not expected.

It was the Monks, the Bards, the Masters of Silence,
Who sat in their caves controlling their thoughts,
Trying to live forever, avoiding death,
Avoiding the need to start over again
    the pain of the illusion called life,
        who were shown the means to escape this tyranny.
They discovered they could place their bodies in stasis
And leave their home worlds
Through the Gates of the Wizard called Merlin.
By that passage they traveled to Arcturus
    and were guided by the Angels to Earth.

Relief! Joy! Exaltation!
One by one they left Orion and lost their tormented selves
    in the mass consciousness of Earth.

At last the tortured had found an existence
That knew nothing of the Plan and even less of their past,
And,
With our blessing, they hid from the Willful Ones,
The Hunters of the departed spirits,
    who would not allow death to release the soul.

Merlin has been, and will remain forever,
The main archetype of the Orion energy
Striving for the integration we seek.
He is the magician,
And his consciousness was born
    through the fusion-collision of polarity,
        not the parity of integration.

He is the wise one.
Created from the differences between slave and master.

He is the spark in the gap when the wills clash.
He has been named as one of the Founders,
But he is more *of* the Source than *from* it.
He is the smoke of the chimney seeking the best path,
Carrying the thoughts of hope
    to a place that welcomes the change.

For you see,
The Orions had been desperate, nothing could help them.
There had been nothing but despair throughout their planets.
Even to hope was cut off from the mind,
For to anticipate good tidings would bring disappointment.
    It was the lack of hope that had created the Merlin.

Forlornness had crept into the Orions' knowing
When it was found
That even in death they were not free.
They came to understand that the spirit
Was immediately trapped upon death
    by the Controllers who monitored the peoples' life force.

Suicide was useless. They were trapped forever.
There was nothing but lifetime after lifetime
Of endless horror, pain and anguish.
It was better to live one long, long lifetime
    than to die and start all over again.

We speak of hell and know not the reality of the imagined.
The Orions lived it and died it.
Year... after year... after year... they lived it.

But a glimmer of awareness came to those who sat
In the silence in their caves of alpha-state.
Someone knocked on the doors of their minds and whispered,
    "Follow me."

Frightened that they had been detected, the Monks ran away.
For generations they ran away.
But the still, small voice followed them.
Finally one day, one Master thought,
"There is nothing to lose."
And he, led by his nose-ring of resignation to the fate
    that the Empire had found his mind to penetrate,

followed the Voice through the terror of the Void
Into the black nothingness of the unknown.

He was led to a light that shone more brightly
Than any he had ever seen before.
He was met by an Angel and was told that Merlin
Could hold open the bridge between Orion and this place,
As long as the passion of despair of the one seeking relief
Could maintain his grip on a single thread of hope.

This Archangel then showed the brave disciple of fate
The planet that would be the healing-place.
Where the spirits of Orion could come, rest and heal
    and in time return to their homeland.
He could help the others whom he had left behind.
Bringing the wisdom he had learned back to the people.
Merlin had shown him the road
    from Orion to Arcturus
        and the Angels to a planet called Earth.

It was magnificent!
After all of those years of suffering,
Here was an opportunity to escape.
It was by way of Merlin!

By Him one could access certain dimensional doorways.
Vortices of the lateral kind
That are anchored in the etheric realm,
Bypassing the Astral plane,
Allowing the movement of the spirit
That was released by a meditation called "Purposeful death"
To move on to a plane that would protect them.

The Monk who was shown the way to escape
Returned to Orion to show others the Gate.
Much like the Shaman who must die
To learn new a paradigm,
    he returned to show the others the way.

They were taught that they could leave
Through Merlin's doorway
    just before the body dies.
They were cautioned that this disappearance

Would create a rift in Time and Space,
Alerting the armada of the Willful Ones,
Who would pursue them through the arc to Arcturus.

The Bards sang:

> "Hurry thou must to the sanctuary of light.
> Tarry not to investigate the unknown.
> The door will be open and the light will be seen.
> Rush to the light else those who pursue thee,
> those who can stop thee from leaving,
> will trap thee and keep thee from reaching thy peace."

Some were caught. Most were not.
They were too fast. Too determined.
And they by their will-driven ecstasy instantaneously
Embedded themselves within our mass consciousness.
Where they would hide in the chaos
Of the disjointed focus of Earth.
And there the spirits of Orion
would forget who they were.

"FREE AT LAST!" they did sing,
as they lost the memory of who they were
and the "Why?" of why they were pursued.
Making Earth's mass consciousness murkier, darker.
Making our nightmares more vivid.
Feeding fear directly to our guts
Where the monsters of the unknown reside.

Making paranoia the god of survival.

And so the Merlin Bridge was established.
Taught by the great Monks of Silence.
And while the trickle exodus was building its momentum,
Another kind of challenge was glimmering on the horizon.
Invited by all of the citizens who could not hold their focus,
As the pain of servitude became too much to endure.

And change it did.

And when it came, the change they invited into their midst
Took the form of the Black League of Resistance.

It grew into cliques of aggressive reformers
Who wrapped themselves in the flag of the Black Dragon.

And they became a league of anarchists
Whose goal was to overthrow the Empire.
To bleach-out the oppressor.
To kill everything that moved with a swagger.

Singlularly dedicated were they to eradicate
Every vestige of domination from their presence.
Seeking to raise up the meek and subservient ones
To take control of their free will and choice.

But they did not reckon that the downtrodden
Would reject their noble plan out of fear of the unknown
And the havoc that unstructured freedom would bring
To their already pitiful existence.

The subconscious had screamed for change.
The conscious cowered at the imagined horror,
"Why trade our known for the unknown?" the sheeple asked.
      "We will wait for our masters to relent.
            They will help us, if only we repent."

Good-meaning, close-minded, and fearful servants
Betrayed the Black League ... over ... and ... over ... again.
And the League became the marauders of terror
Attacking the cities and villages,
Nailing the betrayers and the mind-controllers
On the same crossed pike.
Back to back they were spiked to the post,
With the weak one facing their longed-for home in the heavens,
      the place at the end of the Milky Way.
And the guardian of the mind frying
      in the face of the red-giant ball of death.

In the beginning the Black Leaguers
Were taught by the Masters of Silence
To gather and hold on to their life forces.
They learned the skill of closing down
Their auric field to pure alpha.
Their emotions to pure stillness.
So controlled was their wakefulness
That they absorbed the planet's own energy;
Like a black hole they were,
      and they were never seen.

The Black League's numbers grew
    as individuals were attracted to their cause
        like flies to rancid meat.
They multiplied quietly and discreetly,
Building a force over generations that would in time
    become strong enough to openly fight the Empire.

But they didn't foresee the development
    of technology that tracked heat and motion
        and sensed minor disturbances in the planet's flux.
Their emotions and thoughts were kept in check,
Their breath and their movement betrayed them.

But not before they gave back to the Empire and its citizens
Their own version of what fear of the unknown really is like.
They, by their own mastery of the mind,
Fought fire with fire.
Without mercy they unleashed
    upon the ungrateful population of the meek
        more pain and devastation
            than any dreamt of by the Emperors.

    "It's for your own good you are to be killed," the League
    said simply. "If you are not with us, you are against us.
    You will not be allowed to live to betray us another day."

Sound familiar?

The people, locked in their servitude, died by the sword,
Pleading in their fields and villages for mercy and compassion.
Slaughtered on the spot,
Their blood and flesh became fertilizer for the next rice crop.

The cities of the merchants and the elite
Were surrounded and torched
By the weapons that leaked the electron of death.
By the sonic resonators they opened the ground
And swallowed whole civilizations of wealth.
Great nations were completely obliterated.

Gases were hurled into the plazas and squares,
    catching the Barons and Queens in their beds.
Drugged-groggy they were taken to great vats
    of boiling gold, silver and mercurium

And lowered
   link by link
      into the smoldering cauldrons of death,
And then cast into effigies of wealth.

No living thing could walk on the ashes
Of these civilizations for hundreds of years.
The Black League left nothing behind
   but time-capsuled containers of pox and plague.
Booby-trapped calling cards of their contempt for life.

The League had abandoned all attempts at integration.
Opting instead for war and eradication.
Making Earthlings' purges of genocidal cleansing
   seem puny and impotently boring.

For thousands of years this condition continued.
The war was truly without solution.
For none were changing their minds.

The armies of the Empire were comprised of the people
Who at least understood
That the Controllers and Dream-Walkers
Would not kill them for living their truth.
Life was more important than death to these people.
And the Black League became the mutual enemy.
The liberator was placed in the triad's apex,
Equally opposed by the meek and the powerful.

And watching, maneuvering both sides against the middle
Were the ones We call the Illuminati,
The devious Hidden Masters of the Astral,
Who played both the elite and the weak
   against the heroes of death.

For you see,
High, high up in the Astral planes resided
The mind of the purely self-involved,
Feeding the Emperors with visions of glory
   if they would maintain their oppression of the meek.
The Pure Mind of Evil haunted the nightmares of the people
Who dared to stray upon the path of freedom.
Cloaking its specter in the vision of a snake,
Black as the dragon of the liberators,

The snake of the dwellers of the Astral,
    kept the servants aligned with their masters.

The Astral ones were the mind-consciousness of the great,
    gluttonous,
        Caesarean male whore,
Committed to do anything to keep its own favored advantage
    over all things not of its kin.

Controlling the creation that had been spawned
    on the planets and ethers of Lyra and Vega.
And banished from the realms of Sirius.
Bringing to the people the wrath of the berserkers,
    the evil that they didn't want,
        killing the goodness that Empire needed.

****

The Dawn

The story is now placed firmly at the end of all reason.
The place where no future existed.
The co-creators of all of creation
    had done everything they could to resolve the conflict
And still it persisted.
Like the image in the mirror that looks back unblinking.
Perfectly reversed in every way to its illusion.
180 degrees opposite to needed reality.
Fated never, ever to change.
It is the nature of the mirror to reflect what is given.
It was the nature of Orion to create what was given.

We have carried this conflict within ourselves,
And now it is time to heal and let go.
Power-control continues to struggle
    within the fabric of our knowingness.
It was birthed in the drama of Orion.
Brought to our Earth by those who had escaped
    the life they called death in Orion.
The challenge We have is to accept this knowing
    and melt the bars of our self-made prison.
Just as the Orion has done.

For they now have finally found their freedom.
The freedom that We have been longing for.
It was not by fighting.
It was not by domination.
It was by the blessing of allowance.

The memories of Orion's struggle are rooted within us.
In our dreams We hide and plan;
Conducting assaults with strange weapons and technology;
Playing energy games with those who threaten us.
This is the legacy of Orion,
    brought to our Earth to be resolved in another way.

Daily We work through the memory of THE conflict.
Our polarities muck about within ourselves
And We stumble over the confusion We place in our way.
Not knowing why the anger or the fear is there.
Just knowing that it is; and We think
    that We alone are responsible
        for our deep-seeded paranoia and helplessness.

The Orions brought with them
The antithesis of the Golden Rule,
wherein *"doing unto others, as they do unto you"*
Festers in the gut of Revenge, Resistance and Regret.
Fouling the teaching of *"doing unto others*
    as you would have them do unto you,"
        which lives in the heart of the healer.

The lost ones of Orion are now being found.
They are being invited back to their home.
Great is their suspicion that this is another Empire ploy.
But some have remembered their past
And have traveled to their home world
Expecting the worst and finding the best.
They have returned to Earth and have reported
    that the conflict has been resolved.

"It is over!" they exclaim. "A time of healing has begun!"

"How could this happen?" We ask.

The answer may surprise even the staunchest of cynics.
For there was no solution to the conflict.

So old and anciently inbred it was.
But, one day, there was born
To a great woman Master of Silence,
And a man who commanded the Legions of Black,
Whose uncle was a Prince of the Empire,
One who did not carry the beliefs of his kin.
One who was born to be the embodiment
   of all of the hopes and desires
      of all of the Orion beings.

He was dispossessed of the beliefs of the past!

He was raised in secrecy
And taught by the principle of allowance.
He was given the chance to emerge
   from the shadows of his cave
      to make his way into the world.
To walk alone. Giving no energy to the conflict.
He was not resisting, he simply wasn't playing the game.
And by so doing was able to penetrate
   to the deepest levels of the conflict.

Deep within the innermost sanctum of the people's heart,
He walked and taught
   Love and Light, Life and Law.
The four L's residing within the circle of allowance.

And the Empire's control began to wane.
It had started from the spark that he had brought forth,
Showing the difference between apathy and humility,
   free will and control.
He gave to everyone who heard him speak-think openly
   a glimpse of their ancient right to spirituality and love.
A concept completely overruled and forgotten
   for more than 250,000 lifetimes.

The people blinked.

They began to hear-think and dream freely
For the first time in ages,
   not caring about the consequences of their mind-rebellion.
So tired were they of the Empire's control,
So anxious were they to allow themselves to be free,

That they gifted themselves a vision of a better tomorrow
for themselves and for their children.
The people simply laid down their swords and said,

"No more war.
It is time to breathe the free air.
It is time to plant a flower,
to befriend our neighbors,
and let our oxen relax."

He was like Turtle Brother,
Walking with indifference across the planets of the Red Giant,
Eating what he wanted. Bathing where he wanted.
Not bothering anyone; and by his liberty he taught
The Dragons and the Snakes to keep their fangs sheathed
and allow the people to live.

And the forest fire of allowance spread out of control.

He came because the people were ready.
The critical mass was primed.
One, then two, and then whole groups of people
relinquished the struggle.
They were completely and utterly exhausted
And that in itself was enough to cause others to follow.

He was like the first Master of Silence
who taught the others about the Bridge of Merlin.
He changed their understanding of what was real
and what was not.
He changed the way people would think.

And what happened to Empire?
"What was their reaction?" We would ask.

The Empire dissolved like soda-rock in water.
Some fled to the negative planets of Sirius,
in fear of the revenge of the Liberators.
Others, like the Masters of the Astral,
Were found by the Monks of Silence
and forced to return to the Source
to re-think their positions of control.
Others fled to Earth in their ships of light
as the remnants of the Empire faded from sight.

And the People?
The People, no longer pawns, had learned to accept
The destiny of their own free will!

For you see ...
The Orions were at the brink of extinction.
They were stuck in third density, the yellow-power place,
    and denied the green of the heart.
They were unable to speak the blue,
    to think the indigo, to receive the violet.
They were primed for cellular destruction.
Instant self-ignition created by shutting off the soul.
    Self-immolating spirit-made-manifest.

Orion, was the home of yellow, kept below the green,
by the red-giant Bat-al-juaza, until even He said, "Enough."

    "QAA-LAAS," He said.

And his red began to shift to pink.

"Do it my way or die" is dead in Orion.
Freedom has come on the wings of awareness.
Freedom cannot hide in a cave longing for freedom.
Freedom is.
    Live as freemen and all of reality will change.

It is a new dawn in Orion.
Each morning the sun rises over the planets
And the people feel the love of the Universe
That worked so hard for its awakening.

The Great One taught:

> *Oppression is a choice of the oppressed.*
> *No one country or philosophy*
> *can free you from bondage.*

> *All things done by the governments for the oppressed will fail.*
> *For the oppressed have chosen their position.*
> *All you can do is simply say,*

> *"You have a choice... Nothing is real until you make it so."*

****

Part IX

The Wanderers

We have come to the beginning of the Earth's creation.
Long before the beginning of the story recorded in other books.
But the beginning just the same.

The planet We call home
Became important to a group of Lyrans
When the warring between their cousins and the Vegans
    had become impossible for them to endure.

This group of beings decided
    that they were filled of the violence.
So tired were they of the wars
That they removed themselves
From their homeland and realms
    to wander for ages among the stars.

They were physically and emotionally ill from the stress
Of maintaining their calmer, more nurturing nature
    while war and chaos raged around them.
Like medics they were,
    jumping from emergency to emergency,
        patching wounds and weeping for the dead,
Until they no longer could stand the pain, and they left.
So dedicated were they to service to others,
They left before there were no more others to serve.

Or so they thought.

Because they were more etheric than physical,
Hovering between fourth- and fifth-density realms;
A portion of their being *thought*
    they were more than what they were,
Another part *knew*
    they were far less than what they had become.
The illogical sickness of mind divided against itself
    and its purpose of being
        tormented them.
And they fled from the pain that was killing them.

They had seen their Lyran brethren splice their genes
Into the third-density animals,
Creating cloned killing machines to do their dirty work,
While the bigger minds of control and domination
Could be focused on their enemies, the Vegans,
Who were only doing their thing.
Keeping you and me from enjoying our liberty.

These Wandering Lyrans were of nurturing stock,
And had abandoned their species' cause
    before it had spread to Sirius.
Before it went to Orion.
And they had become the lost children of antiquity.
The first lost tribe of our myths.

They looked and looked for a planet just right,
    far from the clutch of Lyra's influence
Where they could shed their identity and start all over again.

They hated their Lyran heritage.
So ashamed were they of their lineage.

As they traveled from star system to star system,
They seeded some worlds with their Lyran genetics.
Assisting their kin in spreading it around,
Loathing what they were doing just the same.

Then they had decided, No more!

In time they found a new planet emerging
    in the third orbit of a good sun.
It was the Earth they had found.
Isolated,
Tucked away in the protective orbit of a minor sun,
Far enough away from their home worlds in Lyra
To be considered the edge of existence;
They had decided to stop and rest for awhile.

So new was the planet they discovered,
    that they thought they were alone.
But soon they found that it had been reserved
    for something special to become.

Because of its proximity to Sirius,
    they learned of the plan that The Elders had made.

The Wanderers learned that this Sun and its planets
    were reserved for something special.
And, as such, these newcomers,
With their compelling need to nurture,
    were encouraged to stay and to rest.

And they did.

In time they came to name this planet "Terra,"
    and they called Terra their home.
They established seven colonies
Named in honor for their home worlds in Lyra.
They were:
    Maia, Electra, Taygeta, and Alcyone,
      Celaeno, Sterope, and Merope.

They settled into their new home world
    and lowered their vibrations
To be more in touch with the ongoing evolution.
They walked in the gardens, and smelled the flowers.
They tasted the honey.
They swam in the oceans
And frolicked with the dolphins and whales.
They breathed the air
And absorbed its ongoing aliveness-making.
They were at peace with their peaceful selves,
    and enjoyed their freedom
      as they had never enjoyed life before.

And the colonies flourished for a time.

But it didn't last.

After a while they began to notice
That each new generation was feeling
More and more disharmony with the planet.
Their scientists were puzzled at first.
But they soon discovered
That the planet and its beings were evolving.
Beloved Terra's consciousness was changing! Uplifting!
And She was trying to expel their foreign-ness!

They were not indigenous to the planet.
Terra was beginning to change its vibrations,

Making it more difficult for the Wanderers to abide.

At first there were problems with the birthing process.
Soon everyone was discomforted
    by the changes in the planet's electromagnetic flux.
Something had to be done
    else they would be forced to leave!

But this idea was unthinkable!
Leave their beloved Terra?
Terra was their home!

Already, the colony of Merope-Mu
Had vacated their continent in the southern ocean
To be closer to the northern pole,
But even this was proving difficult for them
And they knew that soon they would have to leave.

A congress was convened.
The scientists who had done so much for them,
 extracting nutrients from the planet's coarse vegetation,
spoke:

"We will have to adapt a primate species' genetics in
order to allow our consciousness to become anchored in
the planet's Third plane. Else we can continue to stay for
only a very short while."

The scientists had to raise their voices
    to drown out the unanimous chorus of rejection
        the people made to their suggestion.

"We cannot do to the ape species," the people cried,
"what our Brothers and Sisters have done on Vega and
Lyra. Don't you remember?
"It was because of their manipulation of our home
world's mammals that We left their presence in the first
place! We will not short-circuit the plan of integration by
altering this planet's place in the Universe! We would
rather die first."
"Don't you remember the Elders of Sirius reserving
this planet for healing? We are here to show that We can
resist manipulation of the lower life forms and by our
example We can lead everyone back home. It would be

just as wrong for us to cross-match our genetics with the
reptiles, as the Vegans and Andromedans have done."

And so the debate raged on
Until someone suggested that they do the unthinkable.
This one stood and simply said,

"We have two choices. Stay and die. Or leave and start
all over again. If We stay, We must change. It is not the
planet that has to adapt. It is us!"

Everyone was stunned.
They knew exactly what was said. "We must adapt."
And so another decision, as monumental as the one
That took them from their home worlds, was made.
They decided to take some of Terra's clear primate genetics
And insert them into their own beings!

Deliberately they de-evolved themselves!

Henceforth they would no longer be
     a life form that was pure thought made physical,
They would become physical; more dense,
More susceptible to disease and hunger,
And to their own emotions, which, they found, could kill them.
They would create karmic threads and needs to amend.
They had decided to become an animal!

Do you love your home so much
     that you would become a monkey just to stay?
          They did, and they did.

Now their children were given the chance
To adapt to the changing environment.
The blood they had altered could thicken or thin
In a more natural way;
More attuned to the planet's fluctuations
Of climate and seasons.
Their skin could adapt to the sun's ultraviolet rays.
They became a part of the Earth.
And their transformation lasted for thousands of years.

And then one day they discovered
that they no longer needed the apes' genetics.
They had become terrestrial.

Firmly fixed in the earth's third- and fourth-density spheres,
Able to walk about the planet,
    build their civilizations, live and die,
        write great works, create great music,
And not feel an ounce of discomfort,
Except that which they brought from Lyra.
That pain still remained to haunt them.

The Founders watched with fascination
As the Wanderers had become
The first terrestrial humanoid species!
A model for all to follow.
Complete with the memory of their past
    and able to see into the future.

And the future they saw looked murky
    as the clouds of war spread their way.
The garden of their Eden was being probed
    by both the Lyran and Sirian-Vegan Warlords.

Even though the Wanderers
Had been on Terra for thousands of years
And claimed this planet as their home,
They were not hidden from their more aggressive brethren.

The conflict had spread to Orion.
And because this outpost was so close to Sirius
    and had been colonized by the Wandering Lyrans,
The aggressive ones came to Terra
And claimed it to be a Lyran possession.

Even though they were related to these newcomers
    and knew all the invaders by name,
The Wanderers were repulsed by the presence of their cousins.
And they asked the Lyrans to leave.

    "This is our home. See what We have done? Stay away!
    Please do not bring your war to this planet. She will not
        allow it. We will not allow it!"

Their aversion to war brought forth their weakness.
Their deepest, driven need for peace at all costs.
They were now Terrans and they were unequipped

To repel their aggressive kinsmen,
    who thought nothing of their plan of peaceful co-existence.

    "**S**tupidity," the Lyrans called it. "Nothing more than an
    insult to our Source, our Creator. We have been fighting
for you and all of Creation since the beginning of time. We
    are here to show you the error of your ways!"

Sound familiar?

Was this not the position of the Black League of Orion?
Isn't this the message of all the zealots throughout all time?

    "**W**e've been dying for you for millennia,
        now it is your turn to die for us!"

The Terrans saw immediately that their cousins had not changed.
They were no different than they had been in Lyra.
And neither were the Terrans.

They did not want to fight.
They were technologically outclassed.
They were now less of the etheric and more of the flesh.
They were no match for the Lyran aggressor.
And, even though they knew
    that the Elders of Sirius and the Founders
        didn't approve of these Lyrans and their aggressive ways,
They could not stay.
They were compelled to leave.

By their own inability to reconcile
Their aversion to war of all kinds,
    they abandoned their home ... Again.

By the means of mental war
That their Lyran cousins could wage so well,
And the physical one that the Vegans had mastered,
They were driven away.
They fled from the conflict, leaving their home once again.
Once again denying the darker side of themselves.

But mostly, they said, they had to leave
    because their home and the animals
        were being changed by the Lyrans.
The Lyrans were doing again what they had done before

to all the worlds they had discovered.
The Lyrans were tampering with the primates' genetics!

And the Terrans were repelled by the idea
    of changing the indigenous to suit the "Gods."
They knew that the lower life species
    would never be the same again.
And this, they thought, was contrary to the divine plan.
Not in line with their beloved Terra's fate.

There was no objection felt or heard
    from the great ones in Sirius,
        and The Founders were mute.
Perhaps the Terrans had misunderstood.
Maybe it was better that they leave.

But they couldn't!
They had found that they had lost contact with star travel.
Their vessels were old, made for less-dense beings!
Not physical!
The ships the Lyrans had were faster,
But when transporting physical beings,
Were unable to exceed light-speed.

Even so, they recruited some Lyrans tired of the conflict
Who agreed to take the Terrans to another star system.
Just where, they did not know.
All they knew was that they couldn't continue
The interference, the dabbling and the tinkering
    with the animals genetics.
Nor could they support the Lyran-Vegan conflict in Sirius.

And so they left their beloved Terra
and traveled as far away as they could.

Secretly, they wanted to see their home-star drift
Across their new home's night sky
Just as they had watched other stars back on Terra
Move through the precision of the equinox.

For many generations they traveled through the dark space,
    dying and birthing themselves
Within the thulinium-crystal shells of their flying ships.
Until at last they found themselves

Within the clustered star system of the Pleiades
 and they called this place their home. Again.

And so it was that the Pleiadian culture began,
Complete with an advanced humanoid species
Capable of space travel and the working of miracles.

Good it was that they were so scientifically advanced.
For their beginning was very difficult.
Years aboard their spaceships had caused
Their muscles to atrophy.
Their spines to become lax and spongy.
They were not healthy specimens of flesh and blood.
They had trouble adapting to their newly found homes
Complete with gravity, suns, clouds, and weather.

And they experienced
More of their imbalanced societal growth.

They were the passive Lyrans,
 making Service to Others an acquiescent game.
Unlike their compassionate Nazi brethren,
Who provided the corn, planted the seed and made it rain,
Slave-labored the harvest and then forced the people to eat,
 demanding to be worshiped for their largesse,
The Pleiadians would provide the corn
And show the people how to plant and harvest,
And then would weep when it was not enough.
Wanting to do more,
 restraining themselves from interfering further.

This never bothered the Lyrans, who would do for others
What they should be doing for themselves,
And expected to be honored for it.
An idea that the Pleiadian hated.

Still they were, in the beginning, Lyran,
 and they brought with them many Lyran traits.
One of these was interference,
 which they fervently disliked.
But they couldn't help themselves.
It was reflexive. It is what the Lyran does.
Can a skunk be stopped from spraying?

So the Pleiadians overcompensated
    and stuffed deeper within themselves
        their tendency for aggressive assistance,
Layering another, more murky hue of cultural illness
    over their massive denial of all things negative.

These star-wandering people should have been happy,
They had all the tools to make it so.
Thanks to the Lyran defectors,
They possessed state-of-the-art technology.
They were wise and compassionate.
They were good to one another.
They were everything We would like to be,
Immersing themselves in the amethyst and pink ray
    of Light and Love.
Thinking, above all, that these credos included
    the gold and the blue of Law and Life.

They were wrong.
They were very unhappy, deeply.
And their physical bodies,
Attuned to the chakras that surrounded the heart,
Manifested dis-ease equal
    to their spiritual and emotional denial.

They perceived themselves to be integrated.
But they were in fact living, massive ... self-splitting ... denial.
Rejecting aggression in all forms.
Pushing away, burying deep within their being,
    their "not-so-good-thoughts" and deeds.

You know the feeling. It begins...

        "I cannot Hate this person as much I do! It is not
        healthy. I must Love him ... Ahh ... That's a good
        thought. I'll Love him today, and hope that I can do the
        same tomorrow."

Somehow, this mantra of goodness-making
    is expected to remind us
That hating today can be put off till tomorrow.
That We have helped ourselves purge
An unclean stink from our beings.

Making therapeutically septic our wondrousness.
For We are Gods, are We not?
And what We have done is good for the Soul. Is it not?
A very right thing to do! Is it not?
The ego tells us so.
But it is not.
The Pleiadians,
> by their runaway, abandonment denial,
>> proved that it is not.

Somewhere on that line
> between aggression and submission, We will find
>> the place where Hate and Love become one-confused.
The midpoint called balance.
Like it or not, "dislike" mirrors itself just as Love does.
Radiance and self-loathing are both a state of being and mind.
The mythically real home of knowledge resides
At the place where the Spirit and the Earth coincide.
> The Heart.

Now, We have the Pleiadians,
Who so influenced our lives in the future,
Flourishing, floundering as they created
> the ultimate civilization model.

Utopia.

The one that We would gladly die for.
Trouble is-was, for Us,
Theirs was comprised of One Race, Not Four.
> One skin, Not Five.
>> One Nation, Not Hundreds.
>>> One Language, Not Thousands.
>>> One philosophy, Not Millions.
They birthed themselves a highly philosophical civilization.
Complete with music and beautiful creations of art.
And they continued to live their idea
> of turning their other cheek for generations.

No Master came to them, as they did for Us,
Suggesting another way to behave.
They would have to learn this for themselves.
And in time they were pushed to say out loud:

"**S**omething is not right with our existence."

Their continual suppression of the negative
Had begun to manifest a disease without source.

It came suddenly. They didn't know the source,
They were always so attuned to their bodies.
They could sense imbalance
        and could correct it in a heartbeat.
But this disease was different.
It came out of nowhere and it wouldn't go away.
The people began to die.
Long before their lives were complete, they died.

What they didn't know. What they couldn't know,
Was that the disease came from within themselves!
It was always there, comfortably lodged
Between their etheric and emotional bodies.
Now it was spreading into their flesh and blood,
Their brains and organs and their nerve canals.
It was their own negativity that was spreading!
Their own stuffed, self-loathing and denial was killing them.
And their bodies were doing what they knew best,
Ridding themselves of an unhealthy intruder.

This is all the body knows.
Get rid of the cancer or die!

They were experiencing widespread plagues,
Cancers and viruses like AIDS.
Everyone had been infected-affected.
Be they newly arrived Lyrans,
Or the children of the Wanderers.
And they could not isolate it.

They knew something was wrong.
And because this was so new and they KNEW everything,
They could not bring themselves to believe
That the nonphysical part of their being
Could damage and kill living cells.
They were convinced that they could find the source.
But they didn't.
It was a long, long while before they realized

That their problems were internal and nonphysical.
That there was something they were believing
That was causing the disease to occur.

Because the disease not only affected them physically,
    but also their emotional and spiritual bodies.
Creating voids and gaps within their being
    that nothing could fill.
They discovered that an outside influence could enter
Their previously septic etheric-physical beings,
As tapeworms or parasites would enter our bodies
    through the food We eat or the soles of our feet,
And they were powerless to prevent the invasion.

It was a very low point in their history.
So new and hardly begun it was.
So alone and isolated on purpose were they.
Finally in desperation they called out to their forefathers,
    the Lyrans,
The only people they knew who could help them.
They pleaded:

               "Can you help us?
    We are experiencing manifestations of unbalance.
    We don't know why. We've lived healthy lives.
      We've kept pure our thoughts and actions.
        Why is this happening to us?"

The Lyrans, weary now
    containing a new aggressor, the negative Sirians,
Saw the bigger picture.
They were inspired to show the Pleiadians
What was occurring in the Orion sector of the galaxy.

They showed these peace-loving people
What real massive polarity friction can create.
The Pleiadians looked
    and were horrified by the ugliness of it all.

    "Why can't you do something about it?" asked the in-
credulous Pleiadians. "What manner of beast are you, that
    you could allow this terrible condition to continue?
        "What kind of sickness have you?"

Clearly the Pleiadians thought
    that their Lyran cousins were monsters.
And then they were reminded of what
All-That-Is is all about.

    "Are any of us less capable of understanding our
differences than any of you?" asked the Lyrans. "You are
good people, but you have lost touch with the Law of One.
You have chosen service to others. Not service to self.
Both comprise the Law.

    "The Orions, the Empire, the Black League, and the
peons are battling themselves, just as you are within
yourselves. We have chosen to aid the side that is trying to
reclaim their Liberty. The people of Orion need help, else
they will die, just as you will if you don't quit your non-
example of how to live in peace together. Who's to know
of your existence, if you don't speak your truth?

    "Speak now, Pleiadians! Proselytize! Or waste away in
denial."

So spake the great Lords of Lyra, whom We would know later
    as the Lords and Lord-Gods of Earth.

Thus were the Pleiadians introduced to the Orion war.
Thinking-knowing
That if they could identify the two issues of beingness,
The two ideas that craved to be balanced,
They could somehow bring that knowingness
    into their own reality
        and become filled with health again.

For the first time in aeons the Pleiadians became excited.
They were so excited
    that they charged into the Orion mess
        with their guns and rockets blazing.
They felt sympathy for the people who did not fight back.
They felt aligned with the Black League
    who fought for the peasants.
Not knowing that they had become Lyran-like,
    fighting for the salvation of the weaker people,
        who really didn't want to be helped.

That they out-Lyraned the Lyrans
     would not come to their attention
For several thousands of years.

In the interim,
They were more berserk-like in their battles with the Empire
Than any the Black League had been in thus far.
So crazed they were to save themselves,
They mindlessly killed those they didn't know
     or cared even less about.

Sound familiar?

Better it is to fight a war on a foreign shore.
Better it is to kill those who don't believe as you do.
Better it is to slip into barbaric actions,
     expressing self-loathing thoughts
          upon a Kraut, Jap, Chink, Nigger, or Indian,
Than to kill Aunt Mabel's first-born son, Charlie.
Better it is to hate the enemy than to hate ourselves.

Cowards they were not.
They had all of Time before Time to account for.
They thought that their support against service to self
Would restore their internal harmony.
But it was by the hand of interference
     that they perpetuated their own cycle of disease.
By taking sides and fighting the Empire,
     they supported the Black League
          and continued to fight their negativity.

It just refused to go away.

A thousand or more years later they realized
     that they were no closer to healing themselves
          than they were at the beginning of it all.
This time, however, several generations had been at war.
The new cellular memory traits of aggression
     were making them look forward to the fight.
They were becoming nonpeaceful! More distrustful!
     Less like themselves than ever before.
Nothing was helping them move out of their denial.
They were as trapped in their inability to transcend this reality
     as We are bound in the flesh-mind of our own belief prisons.

Abruptly, they withdrew from the war.
Succeeding only in prolonging the pain and suffering
    that all of the Orion people were experiencing,
Plus losing many of their own kind
    in the Astral-Hell-Life of Orion,
Destined to live and die the pain
    over and over again.

They left. By the cloak of night, they left.

They attempted to slink away from the giant red star.
But the Empire's Armada had been alerted,
By a Sirian-Lyran Overlord spy!
The Armada followed their fleeing ships stealthily.
And when the unsuspecting Pleiadians,
    thinking they were safe,
Had reached the outposts of Electra,
    the Empire's greatest battle Starship, *Wormwood*,
Swooped down and destroyed
    the home planet of their most peaceful sun.
The galactic home of the Council of Light.

The Pleiadians had been defeated
On the doorstep of their civilization; they were defeated
    and there was nothing they could do to retaliate.
The Orions moved with impunity toward
    the more populated worlds of Maia.
And the Pleiadians pleaded for a Truce.
Stalling for time to amass an overwhelming force,
    that would rid the Universe of this cancer forever.

Sound Familiar?

Justice and Goodness were on their side.
Surely the Creator will see that.
After all, We are civilized and they are not....
Over and over this old saw is played,
    and nothing is ever changed.
Until or unless the Creator's Plan-Keepers
    determine that a fresh, new reality can be made.

And so it was.

On the brink of probable annihilation,
    for either the Armada and their death star-ships,
    or the Pleiadians and their whippet-like,
Kamikaze-guided bombs,
The Founders stepped in
And changed the course of the history
    they were about to make.

Changing for us, forever, our expression of beingness.

****

The first inter-galactic Congress was held.
Represented on the soul level were all of the Two-Leggeds.
The mass consciousness of everything that called itself Human.
Everything that was expressing service to self
    and service to others was there.
The Lyrans, the Vegans, The Founders,
    and the Elders of Sirius were there.
The great Angels of Arcturus and Antares were there.

They gathered at the Central Fire, the heart of the Creator.
By their presence and unity of purpose
    they created the Fire and assembled therein.
And the Founders expressed themselves.

> *"The Time has come for the Orions to return to their own worlds*
> *and make their own peace, in their own way.*
> *Long ago, the Elders of Sirius made ready their stars*
> *to embrace the needed healing that others would have to espouse*
> *before all of creation could return home.*
>
> *"They have given much latitude to some of the aberrations*
> *that have occurred within their sector of influence.*
> *There are now in Sirius two distinct distortions of the Law of One,*
> *which are totally different from the two in Orion.*
> *There is a need for an integration place to be established.*
> *This place was identified long ago*
> *and a planet was brought forth from its dormant hibernation*
> *and was placed in the third orbit around the integration sun*
> *and allowed to become*
> *the watery world that it is.*

*"This planet can hold all of the expressions
of carbon-based beingness within its diverse environments.
It will be a new expression of reintegration.
Different from those currently in existence.*

*"We see that the chapter of slave and master
is well on its way to completion in Orion.
The oppressed have found a means of escape,
without the interference of others.
It is time for the war of power to be shifted
and its focus changed.
Death and control over mind and spirit
will end as sentient, deep-density Man
embraces the idea of Love
and accepts the grandness of all forms of creation.
The planet and the place chosen
have been visited by the great spirits of life
and they have found it to be pleasing
as well as having a mind of its own.
That is good.*

*"As some have found,
if one is not in harmony with the place,
the place will cause great discomfort.
That is the Law of Free Will given to all things.
Harmony will always triumph
at the deepest level of being.
Therefore
another chapter of our challenge will be written
on the planet called Earth.*

"The book will be closed there."

The great beings withdrew. The Congress dispersed.
It was decided by one and all
That the drama would be moved to the Earth.
And all of creation would participate.

The Pleiadians were thankful for the reprieve.
They collected the remnants of their fleets
and retreated within themselves.
Once again trying to rectify by their own efforts
their innermost pain and anguish.

They had little interest in the Founders' plan.
It was their beloved Terra that was to be the schoolroom.
Their very first home, ages ago.
All they could see was another kind of Orion misery.

Different, not quite the same. But in the end
    another dead end
        that the Vegan-Sirian-Lyran would muck up, again.
It was not part of their reality to jab a stick in their other eye.

They knew that their Lyran Brothers
    would step up their genetic interference of the young apes.
They knew also that both aspects of Sirius
    would be more active in the planet's development,
        because of the water and reptilian creatures
            that could be seeded there.
By this time the Sirians' knowledge of genetics
    was far superior to the Lyrans'.

Years went by. The experiment forged ahead on Earth.
While nothing much had changed for the Pleiadians.
Their dis-ease continued to control every thought.
And they continued to die indiscriminately.

Finally in desperation they called out again to the Lyrans,

"Can you help us? We are not able to help ourselves."

The Lyrans, unfettered by the belief system
    that tormented their Brothers, said,

"Come back to the Earth that is now forming the new
plan, and we will allow you to be part of the inception
project. This will be of great benefit to you. But you must
provide something for us in return. That something is
your own genetics, which are of the Earth, not the stars.
    "In order to know about negativity you will have to
stay and be part of the planet's development. You may
watch how this planet integrates its polarity. You will
learn vicariously, through the Earth people, how to heal
yourselves."

The incredible arrogance of the Lyrans to suggest
    that the Founders' and the Elders' plan for the Earth

was their own
grated on the nerves of the Pleiadians.
They were THERE when the course was mapped.
They knew the truth and for a moment they hesitated.
Because they saw that if the Founders' vision
Was to become a success,
The Lyrans would take all the credit for themselves
And bluster the triumph over their Cousins.
So incredibly self-serving were they
in their service to others ... themselves.

Nevertheless, they saw too, that they had no choice.
Their species would die if they couldn't overcome
Their own denial of all things negative.
And so,
With heartfelt, gut-wrenching prayers
Sent directly to the Creator, Our Source,
To do the right thing for all of creation,
They agreed to enter the Earth's pageant;
Asking that they be healed
of their self-made deformity of spirit.

And so it was that the Pleiadians returned to the earth.

****

The Wanderers-Terrans were now to become
the Pleiadian-Earthling tamperers of our ancestors.
And with each generation of the Two-Leggeds' development
They loathed themselves even more.
Still they were the primary influence
in the stepped-up program of the Earth's evolution.
This they could not deny.
The evidence waxed greatly in their faces.

But once they were deeply involved in the plan,
They found that they could not resist the calling of the Earth.
And they have returned time and again over the years
to watch the development
of their younger Brothers and Sisters.
Their genetics keeps calling them home.

Earth is their home.
Which by proximity makes Sirius their neighbor,
And the need to protect the planet and its people
Became their Life
    from that time forward.

The Pleiadians. Good people.
Masters of Light, Life and Love.
Trying to integrate the Law of Free Will
    within The Law of Allowance.
Weepingly living an eternity,
    shedding their Judgment of Others.

The Pleiadians,
The first sentient Earthlings when Earth was Terra.
So spiritual and caring were they,
That they purposely de-evolved themselves.
And by so doing they entered the pathos-filled drama
    of growing awareness of their buried denial.
Something We have to do every day of our lives,
Something they had to learn for themselves.

The Pleiadians. Agronomist reformers,
Visitors from the skies,
Myth-born emissaries sent from heaven,
Who taught and loved our ancestors
As only big Brothers and Sisters would.
    As only a grandparent could.
Beloved prophets and teachers were they,
Bringing above all the message of tolerance,
    of love and allowance,
        and nonjudgment to our knowing,
Transmuting our Lyran/Sirian-made genetics,
Thought to assure our ignorance,
    undoing our need for arrogance.

✻✻✻✻✻✻✻✻

Much needs to said about the story of Earth
    that hasn't been said before.
That story shall remain untold until a later time,
    when We look up to the stars
        and see them come down and park on our front lawns.

We will see that the moving stars are but great vessels.
Magnificent ships that bring
   our older Brothers and Sisters
      home for a visit.

They will gather us,
   their younger siblings, all around
      and they will tell us their memory of the time
When Helios and Vesta and Terra (Mother Gaia)
Called out to We the Angels,
And asked us to walk with the Gods in the Gardens of Earth.
The Gods, We forgot, were us.

****

Part X

Mother Earth

And so the Universe turned its eyes to the Earth.
A speck of dust dancing about a minor sun
In a remote corner of the cosmos.
An almost forgotten room in the mansion of the galaxy
Became very important
To everything that ever was and ever will be.

We have come to the place of recognizing our birthright,
And the birth of divergence as it is-was brought to Earth.

It was in Sirius that our planet's need
to integrate its negative and positive halves was born.

It was in Orion that pure selfless and selfish,
the frozen and rigidly unyielding,
rape-and-control-mindedness
Was taken to its ugly but necessary end.

It was in the Pleiades that our future's genetics had festered
in a puss-pocket of denial of all things negative.
Where our craving to reach our fullest spiritual embodiment
was imbedded so completely within our beings.

Where goodness and good deeds
pushed at our frantic need to Love and be Loved,
goading our self-loathing anger to make cruel outlashes
of revenge, resistance and regret.
Making denial an integral part of our spirit.

It was in Earth that the drama would play
the lead role in the reunification of the Universe.
Completely unlike any scripted before.

We The Angels of Lyra, Vega, Sirius, and Orion,
Antares and Arcturus and the Pleiades,
The mythical Two-Leggeds who left the fire
to become separated from our Source of Sources,
our own Heart of Hearts,
have come full circle.
We have tried it all.

The beginning of the end was clearly staked.
Now
    We are only a mind game away from victory.

Earth is the macrocosm of Sirius.
Earth and all of the earths that have ever circled
The GAMMA star of the Elders,
    are the manifesters of the integration
        of this ancient star system.

For you see,
The two stars in the sky We call Sirius A and B
    are in reality
        the ALPHA and the BETA of our beginnings.
The one and the two.
The plus and the minus extremes of our now.
Not just the unity center of a line
That warps through Space and Time,
Being seen like a world flat,
With realms of up and down, life and death,
    with or without,
        but something in between.

Our world is the meat and the wheat of our selfdom.

We have followed the conflict to Orion
And heard the edict of the Founders.
The Hu-Manness part was told.
Now We must seed the story of the Earth itself.
Our blue-green emerald rock of water, mist, and tree
    now firmly destined to be
        the stage, the first page,
            of the last book of the Greatest Story Ever Told.

We need to say something of Mother Earth.

****

She was born in the ice realms of the outer orbits
    of Sirius Alpha and Beta.
The two suns nurtured Her and rounded Her rough edges,
    and taught Her everything She would know,
As She in turn taught them.

Long before the Orion Armada invaded the Pleiades.
Even before the Wanderers had reached our star system,
The Elders of Sirius saw it was time for Mother Earth
    to leave her home
And move to the third orbit of the Gamma Sun.

8.7 light years was Her journey.
And as She traveled, She thawed,
And She moved upward in consciousness,
Awakening to become
    the only water world in this solar system.

For company, She brought with Her a Little Sister.
Not an asteroid or captured meteor-comet,
But a perfect, spheroid satellite
    to light Her dark side during the night.
To be the clock of the Two-Leggeds
    who would soon walk upon Her back.
Little Luna was Her major companion,
    as She grew more aware of Her place amongst the stars.

The Sun welcomed Her
And moved out of Her chosen place close to His warm hearth,
The remnants of another planet that got caught up
In the early power struggles between Master and Slave,
    Good and Bad,
        Right and Wrong.
He expanded the ring of shards and pieces
    and placed them outside of the fourth circle,
Making the fifth ring a rubble-filled moat,
    announcing to all who would come in the future
        that something awry had occurred,
Protecting the inner sanctum.
Where Mercury the Messenger,
Venus the Goddess, and Mars the Warrior
Could watch over our nurturer,
    our Mother the Earth.

The way was now clear for Her.
She would ride the third orbit
    and would learn from the etheric debris
The history of Maldek,

the planet that became suddenly extinct
By the exuberance of the minds of the Atlantis-like Men
who found no room in their hearts to Love their provider.

She basked in the Sun's even warmth.
Luxuriating in His steady heat.
Growing more aware of Her older Brothers and Sisters
who moved in orbits in the dimensions
within, and above, and below Her own.
They were named:
Mercury, Venus and Mars,
Asteroidal-Maldek soon to become whole ... again,
Uranus and Saturn, Jupiter and Pluto
and four others to become known ... again.

They would influence Her course in history,
As They moved through the open sky,
of All-That-Is-Glorious
about infinity's never-ending story,
Teaching Her everything They knew, just as She taught Them.

Today We see the Sun as magnificent,
Warming all parts of our world
three-hundred-sixty-five-and-one-quarter days a year.

Four are the seasons, made by our sun.
Creating life in abundance, if only We could see.

Thirteen are the cycles of Little Luna's Moon-time cleansing,
Marking the passage of time for the Woman-child of the Earth.
Marvelous is the clock of fertility.
Assuring new generations to be birthed.

And We The Angels of our own creation
assured ourselves perfectly
the physicality that We would experience.
We would be challenged to overcome the veil of forgetfulness.
Not so opaquely tight
as the Vegan-Sirian which shuts out all light,
But enough to allow awareness to change
whole paradigms of beliefs overnight.
Where, over the course of history,
one brave one after another

would choose to question the past
or test the waters of the future.

We gave ourselves, our earliest ancestors,
the genes of the gods,
Complete with the gift of the Pleiades.
Their own seven chakras that resonate harmonically,
with the racial differences seeded by others.

Seven are the dancing Sisters of folkloric fame.
Seven are the Sisters of the Pleiades
that wink brightly in our night sky.

And with this gift of our of starry ancestors,
We grew and were encouraged to apply our free will
whenever control squeezed its fist to deny.

We are the Angels. We are the Men of Earth,
and We were given to overcome
all of the challenges of the Universe.

Yes, it was-is painful,
As the cul-de-sacs of bigotry and racial diversity,
False god-worship and empire-builders
Steered the ship of humanity onto the rocks of despair.
Stopping the progress for a Time.
But it had to be.
As All-That-Is needed to experience All-That-Is.
And the Law of Karma-Dharma,
Chaos' gift to the Two-Leggeds,
made sure that its edict was obeyed.

History has turned the pages of time.
And as the upright Two-Leggeds
Grew more aware of themselves,
Our spirits became more firmly joined with theirs
until We were one.

The kundalini-serpent.
The god Kulkulcan was wrapped tightly,
Coiled to flash brilliant insights of more awareness
into the minds of Men.
Pushing the intellect to seek more answers.
Carrying the hopes, dreams and wishes

of all our beloved Creator-Selves,
    one step closer to home.

We brought with us the wisdom
Of everything We had learned and experienced,
And merged it with the Founders' GEM-coded matrices
    buried in the flesh and blood of many Adams and Eves.
Guaranteeing a genetic memory of our Beginnings,
Which will,
    one day,
        open everyone's eyes.

We came to Earth with the charter
First, to heal the philosophies of our past,
    while healing the Earth of our excesses.

Next, to gift ourselves a future
Where We can become aware of ourselves
    and our Earth Mother,
        and our flesh and blood kin, the animals.
Where We can actually sear the wounds,
And heal the scars of our mindless desecrations
Of all things that share our air
In name of avarice, vanity and greed,
And bring ourselves to make complete
    the Circle of the Two-Leggeds
        in the presence of Grandfather Fire.

And then We will make known to our Mother Gaia
    that our arrogance was just our ignorance.
Self-made and proclaimed deliberately for reasons
    our Lyran-Sirian god-selves felt were necessary.

We alone programmed ourselves
    because We had decreed
That We Would Live It And Die it,
    in a good way, hopefully.
Else Mother Earth and her older Brothers and Sisters
Would reject our efforts
    and We would have to start all over ... Again.

Our Mother, the Earth,
    will forgive us our ignorant excesses;

what We have done to Her in our past,
If We, at that precisely correct moment in Time,
Decide together
That We will stop ourselves from taking
   the next predicted step
      that would annihilate the Plan and ourselves.

The prophecies are in place.
The Epics are known.
The Time is now.

****

It began when Mother Earth said to Father Sky,
"I am ready, I am."
She had gathered all the information available
   from the Sirius star system
And stored it within Her crystal caverns
And the chlorophyll of Her leafy hair,
And She waited for our arrival.

We The Angels,
Invited by the Elders of Sirius and the Founders,
Came from the planets and ethers of Vega and Lyra,
Sirius and Orion,
The Stars of the Pleiades, Antares, and Arcturus,
Bringing all of our plans, plants and animals,
Our finely honed genetics to make pure
   racial distractions-restrictions,
To tune the ear and the mind to hear
   voices of different Gods and Lords,
Mucking-muddying the water once so clear
   with just enough impurities to cause
      the logical mind of the self-involved
         to reject everything but what it knows.
To learn the regrets of age and the "if only" of wisdom
   that dies in the exuberance of youth,
      that needs to learn the lesson
         over and over again.
Until wisdom itself spews from the mouth of the child
   and teaches us all
      to live and die in peace.

That is where We are
And the clock stands still waiting
    for the young Man or Woman
        to honor their past and say:

               "We don't need to do this AGAIN."

And MEAN IT!
Knowing WHY.
NOT JUST BECAUSE.

We The Angels came to Mother Earth,
    who had frozen within Herself
        the seedling GEMS of the Universe.
We ate of the Tree to become more of the fruit.
Choosing knowledge over Life.
Thinking that in the end We could have both.
Losing touch with our animal Brothers and Sisters,
    the trees and the insects,
        the part of ourselves that makes all things possible.

Making ourselves ignorant of the time when the animals,
All things large and small, would create for us
    the need to see the differences in our existence,
        and make us question our beliefs and cultures.

Looking forward to the time
    when We can join together in peace.
        To learn how to become Unity again.

It is all a matter of Time.

With or without our presence
Our Mother, The Earth, would make it possible
    for all of us to return home. Again.

But better it is for All That Is
    to be co-creator in our own involvement.
So it is that Mother Earth allows us our arrogance.
And Father Sky allows us to think
that We alone made this reality our Truth.

Sadly, it has taken one cycle of the stars and our Earth
    to complete one sidereal movement of the Universe.

Now, four Hopi Worlds later,
We have returned to the beginning.
We The Angels have returned to the time
When Grandfather Fire heeded the lost Two-Leggeds' call
And infused Himself within Brother Eagle,
  and first stepped upon the Earth.

It is time for us to look up at Brother Raven and call,

"Brother Raven, We are back!
We have so much to tell!"

The End
for now

Epilogue

.... It was Raven who found us. He called out:
"My Brothers, My Brothers, I've found you!
I've found you at last! Come home! Come home!
Make our Circle whole. Again!"....

We looked up and saw this bird who gleamed blackly and We
heard him say,
"*Cqaaawk, Cqawk, Kqaw awh ... Aaaw awh!!!!*"

****

And Raven understood then that he had found us in the Land
of Death, which We, the *Two-Leggeds*, call Life. We didn't know that
We had lost our sacred ability to communicate in the common language of Spirit.

So Raven lifted himself up out of our knowing and returned to
Grandfather Fire. He flew forever. He flew and flew, dragging with
him something that clung to his feathers. It was something uniquely
Hu-man. It smelled. It hampered him. It was sweet in its decay.
Ripe without life. It burdened him, and he tried to rid his splendrous
feathers that once had shone so brilliantly silver, of the black sticky
stuff of Hu-manness.

He cleaned himself, cat-like as Brother Panther would. But he
could not rid himself of the sticky stuff that We know as the dark
side of emotion: sadness and despair.

He flew with the sticky decay in his beak and found that with
every wing-beat, he was diminishing his own life-force. That he
was getting weaker. Something was happening to him. He was
still ages from finding Grandfather Fire, his Brothers, his Sisters.
He felt a twinge of another emotion. It was fear. And it drew even
more life-force from him. Brother Raven became weaker and flew
lower in the Darkness.

Almost home now. Raven flew with the weariness of our ancient ancestors. The ones that carried the burdens of the Worlds
upon their backs. The Sticky Stuff now had grown so great upon
his feathers that it began to smell from within him. It now covered

every single sliver of silvered feather with its decay. Lower he dropped, now no higher than the tallest tree on the highest mountain, and saw Grandfather Fire! At last he was home! "My Brothers, I am home!" He collapsed on the ground, exhausted from his journey.

They came to him and nudged him. But he smelled different! He looked different! He was not Brother Raven. He was someone else. He had changed. His feathers were as black as the Darkness of the Night. Brother Raven got up and went to Grandfather Fire to tell Him and his Brothers the story of his journey.

Raven had returned to the Circle of Animal Brothers and had told where he had found the *Two-Leggeds*. He then passed around the Stickiness so that each in the Circle might feel it, smell it, and taste it. Soon they were discussing amongst themselves what should be done about their Brothers, the *Two-Leggeds*.

"Now that we know where they are, we have to bring them home," said Brother Panther.

"No, we can't do that," answered Bear. "They left on their own."

"We've got to bring them home, they're our brothers. We have a responsibility towards them," said Deer.

"Yes, but what of their responsibility towards us?" asked Turtle.

"We can't just leave them out there," pleaded Gander.

"What are they doing out there, leaving us alone?" asked Snake.

"How is it that they got out there? Why is it that they're there? Why would they do such a thing and break our Circle?" asked Horse.

It was all so confusing.

Grandfather realized that creation was changing again and something must be done. He thought and thought and finally He said to Eagle, *"Brother Eagle, you are the grandest of all of my creations. I will place my own presence within you and you will return along the pathway found by Raven. We will see what is to become of the Two-Leggeds."*

The Circle of Animal Brothers agreed that this was a fine idea. And so, Grandfather Fire infused His own presence into Eagle and sent Eagle forth into the darkness, following the trail left by Raven. In less than an instant, Eagle had passed through the Gates of Death into the land of the *Two-Leggeds*. And as his Eagle talons touched the Earth, He took on the form of a man. One whom We call Eagle Brother/ First Shaman.....

****

One thing We will have to learn
before We can hope to go home,
is that all of Creation are co-creators with us.

The Founders and the Elders are part of the story.
Mother Earth and the planets are another.
The animals most certainly make our lives possible.
The insects and plants have contributed their lives also.
Life-begetting-life in a give-away manner.

Nothing stands alone.
Not one thing lives or dies unnoticed.
That is the beauty of our Source.
The magic of our dream.

Our reality was allowed to gestate
in the nurturing vat of a water-based world,
amidst the desert-like planets that circle our Sun.

By Little Luna's example of enlightenment-making,
waxing and waning in cycles,
We can always acknowledge our spiritual selves,
and show by baby-stepped growth
that divineness is our goal.

Sirius was the home of our true beginnings.
First was Lyra, Vega and the Apex.
Precursors of the need for polarity's meld.
The wars of correctness spread to Sirius Alpha and Beta
and then were placed in exile in Orion.

How many Law-and-Lifetimes have to be repeated
before Light and Lovetime is known?

The clock of evolution and karma marches incessantly,
with the Moon and the Sun marking the seasons,
with Mother Earth and our kindred beings making it all possible.

And so it was that the Earth
was slowly warmed and life began to stir.
Guardians from Sirius came to watch over the development.
The Wanderers came and were given leave to stay.
The Lyrans came and drove the Terrans away.

Then the Founders made known the agreement
between the Elders, the planets and the suns of Sirius.
The Empire of Orion returned to their home worlds,
And the Earth began the final chapter of the Universe.

.... *to be continued*

Howard Reed
Flagstaff, Arizona

****

Selected Bibliography

The telling of "The Circle of Animal Brothers" as related by Jade Wah'oo, Shaman of Lineage *Shaman's Dream*, Act II, Chapter 3, "Sorcery or Shamanism?" Unpublished. Used by permission.

Lyssa Royal, Keith Priest, *The Prism of Lyra*, Royal Priest Research, 1992.

Royal Priest Research/Lyssa Royal, *The Earth Inception Series* (nine cassettes), 1989.

Don Elkins, Carla Rueckert, James Allen McCarty, <u>The Ra Material: An Ancient Astronaut Speaks</u>. Virgina Beach, Va.: The Donning Co. Publishers, 1984.

Don Elkins, Carla Rueckert, James Allen McCarty. *The Law of One*, vols II, III and IV. L/L Research, 1988.

Families of Consciousness material from: Jane Roberts, *The Unknown Reality, A Seth Book*, vols. 1 & 2. Englewood Cliffs, N.J.: Prentice-Hall, 1977.

For Information about "The Starseed Mandala" illustration on the cover contact: Gage Taylor & Uriel Dana, P.O. Box 2163, Sausalito, CA., 94966, e-mail: Sirius_Art@ aol.com